Playing Outside

Making outdoor teaching and learning work in practice is a key priority for all early-years practitioners.

Playing Outside provides clear and detailed guidance on all aspects of outdoor play. Including over 100 full-colour photographs, it practically demonstrates how you can create an environment outdoors that facilitates long-term projects for children that support their learning and development. This new edition has been fully updated throughout with new photographs, case studies and ideas for resources to enable you to make the most of your outdoor area.

Helping you to encourage children to concentrate, persevere and develop their thinking and social skills, while promoting physical activity and a healthy lifestyle, the book features:

- practical activities that cover all aspects of learning;
- discussion of the role of the adult in making outdoor provision successful;
- colour photographs illustrating good practice and imaginative use of equipment;
- examples of work from a range of settings; and
- help and advice on suppliers of equipment.

Written for all practitioners working in schools, nurseries and pre-school settings, this book is essential reading for those who wish to provide inspiring outdoor play opportunities for the children in their care.

Helen Bilton is Associate Professor in Education at the University of Reading.

Playing Outside

Activities, ideas and inspiration
for the early years

Second edition

Helen Bilton

Routledge
Taylor & Francis Group

LONDON AND NEW YORK

Second edition published 2014
by Routledge
2 Park Square, Milton Park, Abingdon, Oxon OX14 4RN

and by Routledge
711 Third Avenue, New York, NY 10017

Routledge is an imprint of the Taylor & Francis Group, an informa business

First edition published by Routledge 2005

British Library Cataloguing in Publication Data
A catalogue record for this book is available from the British Library

Library of Congress Cataloging in Publication Data
Bilton, Helen.
   Playing outside: activities, ideas and inspiration for the early years/
Helen Bilton. – Second edition.
   pages cm
   1. Outdoor education. 2. Outdoor recreation for children. 3. Education,
Preschool. 4. Play environments. I. Title.
   LB1047.B53 2014
   371.3'84 – dc23
   2013030680

ISBN: 978-0-415-60480-2 (pbk)
ISBN: 978-1-315-81866-5 (ebk)

Typeset in Bembo and Helvetica Neue
by Florence Production Ltd, Stoodleigh, Devon, UK

Printed in Great Britain by Bell & Bain Ltd, Glasgow

Contents

Acknowledgements

Thanks go to the following, who helped with ideas and images:

Anne Crook and Chilton Primary School

Diane Lister and Slough Centre Nursery School

Helen McAuley, Elizabeth Spendlove and Balham Nursery School

Helen McHale and Maidenhead Nursery School

Jenny Stephen and Boyne Hill Infant and Nursery School

Nicky Turner and Christ Church and St Peter's Church of England Primary School

Sarah Cottle and Cookham Nursery School

Val Thomas and Wessex Primary School

Introduction

Playing Outside is the second edition of a book written in 2004. Much of the content is the same; children and their needs do not change! All the images are new and collected from schools running and managing their outdoor teaching and learning environment, never standing still but striving to do the very best for their children.

The emphasis in the book is of ensuring we create an atmosphere that supports long-term projects for children, particularly so they can really develop thinking and talking. In this way, children can be encouraged to concentrate, persevere, think through and succeed in their endeavours, all the while talking and listening. To demonstrate this approach, a number of the images are of projects over time. A small-scale research project found that although children are wishing to be involved in conversations of depth and meaning, staff members do not support this as they should (Bilton 2012).

The book is divided into five chapters. Each chapter discusses the issues and provides ideas, photographs, case studies and questions to ask. Chapter 1 discusses the reasons for having outdoors, and how playing and working outside can impact very favourably on children. Chapter 2 considers why and how the adult's position is critical in making outdoor provision successful. Chapter 3 demonstrates how the whole curriculum can be provided outside. It includes resource lists, ideas and issues to consider. Chapter 4 discusses the broader issues that can make or break success outside. Chapter 5 shares the stories of those who have made changes, or are working with older children. The final part offers resources and contacts, and useful books.

1 Do we need the outdoor environment?

Any educational experience is made of the who, the what and the how; that is, the children (who), the curriculum or knowledge (what) and the environment (how). We have to be convinced that children will gain from an educational experience, so in this chapter, I will be putting forward the case for providing the outdoor environment. How we bring children and knowledge together is crucial in making the educational experience worthwhile. Done badly, outdoor play does little for any child; done well, outdoor play can help and support children as they think, feel and act.

Figures 1.1–1.11 Children active, absorbed and purposeful.

This series of photographs shows a group of children moving a large mound of bark chippings to create a new play space. This activity lasted the whole afternoon despite the miserable weather. A number of children were fully engaged for the entire time and others joined for shorter periods of time, sometimes returning later. Both boys and girls were involved. At times, the teacher was involved, and at others, she was standing back. Children learned to manoeuvre spades and wheelbarrows, cooperate in terms of space and equipment, balance on the mounds, consider and discuss the next steps, help others and our school class, be responsible and, most importantly, use language in a meaningful context and learn new language. Children danced, ran and slid.

The children were practising dispositions needed to be successful in the educational setting and society – perseverance, consideration, concentration and curiosity. Katz has strongly argued for a long time that children can learn, and seemingly achieve, when given academic tasks, but that unless they grasp the dispositions for learning, the skills will wane (Katz and Chard 1989). Why bother about science if you do not have the disposition of curiosity? Lastly, this activity did not need specialist or fancy equipment, and it had not been created as an activity to fit the curriculum. It was part and parcel of the 'everyday' of that class. The best and most effective classrooms are ones where these work activities are seen as learning experiences. It did not require workmen to move the bark, because the children were taking responsibility for their garden.

The adults did interject at critical times, to ensure play continued. Two children were throwing the bark chipping near a drain and the adult suggested using the water tray to put the bark in. Two children were arguing about a tyre and the use of it, and the adult suggested getting another one. They did and played well, but two terms ago this would not have happened.

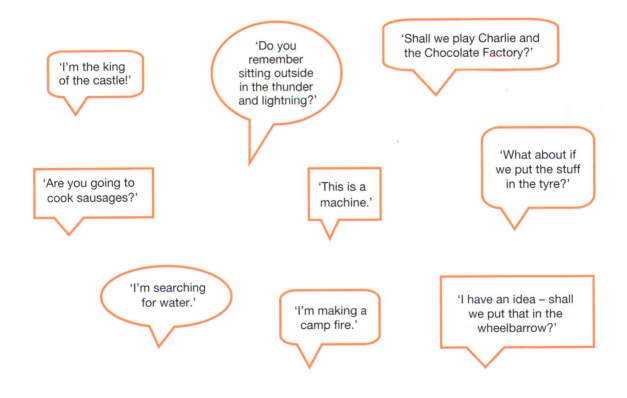

Figure 1.12
Some comments while moving the bark chippings (see Figures 1.1–1.11).

Three reasons for having outdoor play

Reason 1

Outside is a natural environment for children; there is a freedom associated with the space that cannot be replicated inside.

If children feel at home in a particular space it seems logical to teach them in that area; education should not be a chore, but an enjoyable and worthwhile occupation. Ask any grown-up about their childhood and a glazed expression will come over them when they talk about going outside to play! They talk in terms of doing their own thing, staying away from grown-ups, spending lots of time with friends, negotiating and cooperating to make things, having and sorting out arguments, having fun, getting really worn out and just simply relaxing. Outdoors is somewhere most children like to be, but it needs to be enjoyable, fun, relaxing and involve others. The grown-ups mention learning in terms of learning about being with other people and learning how to give and take, understand and forgive. Grown-ups do not often mention the formal curriculum, but they will have learned about every subject area of life. They will have learned to be self-reliant, to take risks, but not put themselves in danger when jumping a stream or climbing a tree. They will talk in terms of understanding the weather, reading the change in atmospheric conditions, a part of the science curriculum learning. Through dividing children, stones, etc. into groups, they would have been putting into practice the multiplication tables.

If you ask children who controls the home, most say the mother; to the question who controls the classroom, it will be the teacher; but when asked who controls outside, children will say no one. If that is the case, then one cannot be judged in that space, hence why children might feel more comfortable in this environment. If they cannot be judged, then they have a freedom to be their true selves and to take risks where failure may be possible, but where they will not be condemned for it.

Case study

William, aged 9, said, 'Sometimes I feel really itchy and spiky when I get home from school and not very nice, but if I go outside, then I feel OK again and I am not horrible to anyone.'

This child knows how he feels in different environments and how that then impacts on people around him.

Reason 2

The environment in which children and adults play and work can affect their emotions, behaviour, personality and ability to learn. To give you a perspective of this, envisage the underground in London. Some people like it, some do not. Some feel claustrophobic, some love looking at all the different people. So that is an emotional response; this then affects the behaviour of the people, whether they are furtive or bold. This can, in turn, dictate whether they get to their destination with ease or not. So then we think of outside, another environment, and not only do children react differently to it in comparison to inside, but in comparison to each other. Some may feel more confident outside, some more creative, some more vocal. So looking more specifically, how are children affected by being outside?

Figures 1.13a–1.13c
Writing material is available at all times, so writing is just part of the play, naturally.

- Some children prefer to work and play outside. Certain children seem to prefer to play inside, some outside and some seem able to utilise both areas. However, even those children who prefer to play outside, given good inside and outside areas, will utilise both, but the inside area to a lesser extent. Traveller children, and often refugee children, may prefer to be outside, as this is where they naturally live for most of the day. For them, they *need* to be outside, as this is where they feel empowered.

- Some children are less inhibited outside. You can find in a setting one child with two personalities, one associated with inside and one outside. Inside, a child can be reticent, shy, unwilling to get involved with many of the activities. However, outside, the same child can be vocal, effervescent and perfectly happy to have a go at any activity. It would appear that the affecting force is walls and a ceiling; this is sufficient to affect the child's whole personality.

- Some children are more able outside. Outside play for some children can involve more mature discussions, more advanced play and more ability. For me, the very crucial issue is that if these children are tested/judged/assessed outside, they would be found to be more able than if they were judged inside.

- Some children are more assertive and imaginative outside. Being assertive means being able to put one's ideas or points of view forward, and being confident enough to take a lead role in the play; this can only occur for certain children if they are playing in an outdoor area.

- Some children will use activities placed outside that they would not use inside. Some children can feel reticent about books and writing and, for some, there is a greater risk to putting pen to paper than climbing a 10-metre fence. When books are placed in an environment that children feel secure in, they are able to access them. Some girls can feel reticent about construction play inside, but happy to get involved when the resources are outside. For others, it may be painting or role play. Older children tend to prefer to play imaginatively outside and will not access this type of resource inside (see Figures 1.13a–1.13c).

- Some children can concentrate and persevere for longer outside. There is some suggestion that boys' activity spans can be longer outside than inside and longer than girls' spans outside. It would appear that adults differ in where they can concentrate: some need total quiet, others seem to cope with interruption, and likewise children are different in their tolerance levels. To concentrate, we need to be interested in the activity, happy with the space we are working in and aware that mistakes are okay. For some children, this type of atmosphere is only prevalent outside.

- Some children will learn more outside than inside. It would seem to follow that if children feel able, secure and confident, they are likely to learn more than if they are feeling unable, insecure and lacking in confidence.

Reason 3

Outdoors is a perfect place to learn through movement, one of the four vehicles through which children can learn, the others being play, talk and sensory experience. However, for learning through movement to truly work, there needs to be enough space to move, do and find out. Learning by doing may involve pulling a truck, digging or arranging blocks in a particular space. All of these activities need enough space to be worthwhile. Through activities such as these, children will not only learn and find out many concepts and learning attitudes, but they will also benefit from becoming healthy and staying so. It is so very important for children to be vigorous in their movements, to the extent that the heart and lungs are working hard, and they

Case study

Sulmah was a shy and reticent child when she started nursery at age 3. Her first language was Urdu and she was working in English outside the home and community. She stayed with one particular member of staff for the first few weeks at nursery, and would only go outside if this staff member was with her. She tended to wander and watch but not partake of activities, even though the staff member tried to encourage her. One day, a huge colony of wood lice and one stag beetle were discovered in the 'minibeast' area. This seemed to be the catalyst for Sulmah; she was absolutely fascinated by this discovery and stayed watching them for around half an hour, leading on to drawing a variety of the insects. The next day, Sulmah strode outside without the staff member to watch the insects in the 'minibeast' area. This was followed by a strong desire to communicate verbally with staff members about the happenings in the 'minibeast' area, and her confidence from that day grew and grew. Through this experience, it seems Sulmah found the confidence to communicate and act; she may have had an experience inside that would have created the same spark, but she may not. This outdoor experience affected Sulmah emotionally, linguistically, and therefore intellectually.

get out of breath. The activity needs to be daily and simply part of the routine of the day; children who experience activity as part of their day tend to go on to adulthood in the same vein. Exercise can also affect emotions, allowing for relaxation and calmness and a heightened sense of well-being. Added to this is the impact of fresh air and light outside. If we look at the research of Clements-Croome *et al.* (2008) from the University of Reading, they found that in classrooms where the CO_2 level was high, children's ability to function optimally was affected adversely, reactions slowed up and memories were affected. Likewise, children need light; vitamin D regulates the amount of calcium and phosphate in the body and is vital for healthy bones. But the vitamin is activated under the skin in reaction to sunlight. If vitamin D is not activated, then children can suffer from rickets. Outside can be more peaceful than some classrooms, and everyone needs peace and quiet. Research from Shield and Dockrell (2008) found that excessive noise had a harmful impact on children, whether inside or outside. And the impact on children with special educational needs (SEN) was even greater.

Conclusion

So, yes, we do need learning and teaching to happen outside, so that all children can work in an environment they feel secure in, whatever the activity. Children in a good outdoor area will appear active, absorbed, motivated and purposeful – a very satisfying sight!

Questions

- What do children say about the outdoor area?

- Ask the children who they think controls outside.

- Have you noticed any differences in the children's behaviour, personalities or actions outside in comparison to inside?

- Does outdoor provision reflect what is going on in the children's lives?

- Do you assess children outside?

- How often do the children get out of breath?

- Do children rush to get outside? If so, what is wrong with the inside provision?

2 The adult's role before, during and after outdoor play

Rather than 'do to' children, remember 'do with'

Children need freedom outside, but they do not need a free-for-all; it is the adult's job to make sure all children can learn, enjoy and reach their potential. You 'reap what you sow': if outside consists of a few bikes, a climbing frame and disinterested adults, then it is likely that the children will argue about the few toys, not learn very much and feel dissatisfied when they go inside. They may also feel hurt and confused by the attitude of the adults and react poorly when they return inside. So then, the outdoor ethos impacts adversely on the inside atmosphere. If you provide quality outdoor teaching and learning, children will become confident, independent and learn a great deal.

Figure 2.1
This adult is a part of this child's world. She is interested and concerned for the child to do well.

The Effective Provision of Pre-School Education (EPPE) research

revealed that where settings viewed educational and social development as complementary and equally important, children made better all round progress. Effective pedagogy includes some structured interactions between adults and small groups of children, traditionally associated with the term 'teaching'. Also notable in more effective settings was the provision of planned learning environments and 'sustained shared thinking' to extend children's learning. Trained teachers were most effective in their interactions with children, using the most 'sustained shared thinking' interactions. Adults in excellent settings had a good grasp of the appropriate 'pedagogical content knowledge' knowing which curricular content was most relevant to the needs of individual children. This required a deep understanding of child development.

(Sylva *et al.* 2012: 5)

So what is being said here is that, in essence, adults need to be very knowledgeable about child development, interested in the children in their class and able to put the two together (see Figure 2.1). Below are some thoughts about how adults working with young children need to be in order to be successful with young children.

Staff with a positive attitude

Staff members need to be supportive towards outdoor teaching and learning! If the whole staff group wants to use outside effectively, this is half the battle, but this is not always the case. One way of getting staff on board is to look objectively at what is happening outside and to identify the problem areas. The analysis of practice pro formas (Tables 2.1 and 2.2) can help with this. To use Table 2.1, in the left hand column, list the areas of the space (in and out) (for example, book corner, construction, role play and so on). Then, every five minutes, simply write the initials of the children in that area. This can also be done for the adult involvement, so list which adults are where. The more often you make the observations, the more rigorous the research will be. So you could decide over a 3-week period to observe 3 times a week for 30 minutes. In this way, you can find out:

- who (children and staff) is moving about a lot;

- who (children and staff) is staying at certain activities for a long time;

- who and with what the staff members are working; and

- which areas are not being visited by children or staff.

Then one needs to analyse the information. If a very young child is flitting about, it probably is not a problem, but could be if the child is older. If a child is staying at an activity for a long time but able to incorporate all aspects of the curriculum, then that probably does not matter. But if the development of the child is being hampered by staying in a 'comfort zone', then the child needs to be helped to discover the whole curriculum within the setting. 'Comfort zone' mentality can be quite prevalent in some settings where an understanding of child–initiated activity is not grasped. Some children, day in, day out, stay within one area, zone or activity. Or, at least, for the majority of the time. It can be a girl or group of girls and the writing area, or a boy or group of boys and construction. This is all fine as long as the child has the opportunity to practise and develop in all areas of the curriculum. If they go to the sand tray every day and stay there for an hour, with minimal interaction from adults, and what is in the sand has little

Table 2.1 Involvement analysis

Activity	5 mins	5 mins	5 mins	5 mins	5 mins	5 mins

Table 2.2 Demand schedule

Type of demand	Number of demands in a 20-minute period
To play	
To explain	
To have a conversation	
To find something	
To help	
To mend something	
To celebrate something	
To deal with disagreements	
To answer a question	
To ask permission	

Key

Play – when a child specifically asks an adult to play with them

Conversation – when a child simply comes for a chat often about their life, what they have been doing, going to do

Help – when a child is making something and needs an adult's help. This is very often to hold something

Show – when a child needs to celebrate a product or process

Question – where a child is involved in learning and requires an answer, 'Why has that changed colour?', 'Why is the water moving?', 'Why won't these stay in?'

Explain – to show why something has happened, regarding what they are doing now or have found out in the past

Find – where an adult is needed to collect resources which a child cannot reach, or is not allowed to take

Fix – to mend something which has come apart or broken

Disagreement – where children are in disagreement and need adult assistance whether it be over a resource or toy, but not about a fact

Permission – where children are expected to ask to go to the toilet, to collect coats, change activity

to do with scientific development, then the child is being severely disadvantaged. First, the resource needs to be much improved; second, the adults need to be involved with the child and his or her development; and third, an audit needs to be made of that child to see if he or she is having opportunities to draw, paint, interact, discuss and so on. If no one is visiting an area or learning experience, then you need to ask why and do something about it. Get the staff working in that area, or redesign the area, or relocate it. Or, if none of these work, remove the activity.

Table 2.2 is to analyse why children are coming to adults and what the interactions entail. In a 20-minute period, and this can be repeated over a few weeks, note down why children approach the adults. Is it to play, share a discovery, ask for a bike, go to the toilet, or complain about someone else? We should be having interactions of depth and meaning, not low-level 'domestic' conversations.

See Bilton (2013a) for more discussion about child–initiated activity outside.

Planning

Outside is a half of a whole, with inside being the other half. It is much easier to plan if the two areas are seen as integral, not separate. If the two environments are viewed together, then the planning can be viewed as such. Nicholson (2001) suggests incorporating outdoors in the plans for indoors, so only one document is needed, outside activities complementing indoors and vice versa (see Tables 2.3a and b). By combining the planning, one can also consider the best placement of a resource or activity, thereby maximising the learning. Some planning simply lists resources or fixed structures with no indication of learning possibilities, skills or attitudes to be taught. However, it is more effective to note down what it is you are trying to achieve with the children, the actual activities to be carried out and questions to be asked. In this way, the learning can take place anywhere and a climbing frame can be a den for rabbits one day and the base for a scientific test the next. Table 2.4 is an example of planning for child-initiated activities or activities that have been set up without the need for constant adult presence. Note how the actual questions to be asked are listed. Note how the clay activity is built upon over the week – getting away from this idea of having to put something new out every day, with no link to observations. There are many ways to plan; the case studies offered here are not given as definitive, but to provide ideas. It is impossible to actually demonstrate the amount of discussion that will go on before and after the planning, but for planning to work, there has to be a reasonable amount of time devoted to discussions.

Case study

Slough Centre Nursery School felt that not all their children were getting to know outside well and so they put into play that every home group over a week would start their day outside and meet and greet the parents there, and those children would simply naturally be outside and would start to play there. The parents were also made more aware of the need to dress their children appropriately (see Figure 2.2).

Table 2.3a Example of medium-term planning

Medium-term planning	Start date:	Expected end date:

Theme: Minibeasts

Personal, social and emotional development

Broad learning intentions
To understand the need to care for living things
To show interest and involvement
To persist in looking for living things
To collaborate and share learning with others
To look to others for support in learning

Key activities and starting points
Set up a minibeast environment outside
Set up an inside minibeast area, having observed outside
Encourage children to share knowledge and observations
Paired activities – one observes and the other draws
Set up a science resource base
Read *The Bad Tempered Ladybird*

Communication, language and literacy

Broad learning intentions
To use increasingly descriptive spoken language
To record observations with pictures and writing
To use resource books, tapes, videos and CD-ROMs to access background information
To learn and devise rhymes, poems and songs about small creatures

Key activities and starting points
Resource display of books etc.
Dictaphone tape recordings
Children preparing talks on what they have seen
Use insect big book outside and to support talks
Provide minibeast key word cards in writing area
Set up role-play animal hospital

Creative development

Broad learning intentions
To observe and respond to minibeasts through movement, art and craft, music and play
To express and communicate a wide range of outdoor experiences

Key activities and starting points
Make minibeast puppets and develop a series of shows
Make and provide dressing-up clothes: ladybird, spider, butterfly
Make a collection of instruments for minibeast music
Sing 'caterpillars only crawl'
Use wire and moulding materials for minibeast sculpture

Physical development

Broad learning intentions
To use scientific equipment with care and control
To handle a wide range of small apparatus
To give thought to whole-body movements
To develop the confidence to climb and crawl
To be aware of hygiene when in contact with minibeasts and their environment

Key activities and starting points
Provide tweezers, droppers, nets and teach correct ways of using
Extend the outdoor small equipment range – add small balls and bats
Use play frame imaginatively to move in response to insect observations

Mathematics

Broad learning intentions
To count in a variety of contexts
To calculate with numbers with which children are confident
To look at shapes in the natural world and recreate
To investigate measuring of length

Key activities and starting points
Count and tally numbers of insects in log pile
Measure worms!
Make plasticine worms of particular lengths
Use magnifiers to find and describe shapes in creatures
Minibeast calculating games (home-made)

Knowledge and understanding of the world

Broad learning intentions
To make observations and record verbally
To make observations and record with pictures and models
To make suggestions based on observations
To recognise some of the conditions some creatures prefer
To use CD-ROMs to find extra information
To select a range of resources independently

Key activities and starting points
Set up a range of environments outside and inside
Provide a bank of books and CDs
Make a collection of sound recordings of our observations
Visit to retillary at Syon Park to see creatures from other places in the world

Source: Nicholson, 2001.

Table 2.3b Example of short-term planning for both inside and outside

Short-term planning

Week beginning:

Learning intentions — What do we want children to learn?	Activities, experience and language — What do you want children to do?	Resources — We need:	Links	Children	Comments — What have they learned? What next?
To show interest, involvement and perseverance To know that we need to take care of living things	Look at log pile with small groups and magnifiers Provide small pots and bug viewers Provide clipboards and paper close to log pile	Log pile Pots Viewers Collection of magnifiers	K & U	Rahena Rubina Tommy Jody Mustafizur	
To be able to talk about what is seen at the time and later To use descriptive language To listen to others and ask questions about what they say To record observations with adult support	Adults to lead investigations talking about the need to be careful and gentle Talk informally about their observations and thoughts with other children on the mat Introduce 'Insect Body Parts' big book – focus on magnified pictures Adult-supported drawing and writing in writing area	'Insect Body Parts' book	K & U	More confident speakers	
To use language, e.g. longer, shorter, the same, when making comparisons To recognise that long things are not always straight To count objects that cannot be moved	Use clay, plasticine and playdough on different days to make model of what has been seen Make worms of various lengths and play games guessing which is the longest and shortest Count the insects collected in pots at the log heap – who has the most, least? etc.	Clay Plasticine Playdough Fabric Cord String Paper strip roll		All children but in two small groups	
To make observations using magnifiers and viewers To understand magnifiers make things appear larger	Provide various magnifiers inside with various things to look at – including text and pictures	Photographs of creatures that have been enlarged	C D K & U	All children Group 1 and 2 Group 3 and 4	
To handle magnifiers appropriately	Set up instrument collections, e.g. scrapers, twisters and tuned percussion, to respond freely to observations of minibeasts through music			Nusrath Joshua Milo Available to all children – support less confident	

Source: Nicholson, 2001.

Table 2.4 Example of planning for and assessment of self-initiated activity

University of **Reading**

FOUNDATION STAGE
Self Initiated Activities (can also be used if adult sets up these areas)

Area/Activity include Resources/Equipment	Possible questions, explanations	Learning intentions/ areas of learning	Who used area and how, including extra equipment brought in	Learning, under-standing, and talk	Next steps, in terms of provision/resource and children's learning
Clay, on own, in small balls on separate wooden trays, each day add new resources dependant on children's work – tools, water, ideas.	What does it feel like? Can you make it into a ...... shape? Can you roll, poke, squash, squeeze, punch, stretch, flatten it?	To discover a new material and to explore its potential. To develop language associated with the feel of the clay.	Huge amount of interest expected and particularly from older children, including boys. Some children wanted to use tools which actually negatively affected play.	Initially quiet, adult presence needed to encourage the exploration and to reassure that the clay would wash off. J–inspired to talk – quite forceful with the clay, and used clay to story.	Continue with just the clay, needs more exploration with hands only. Work with J and bring in S and D who were on the sidelines but not quite confident to come to table.
Water–catching air bubbles. Water tray, various flannels.	That's amazing! Why is that happening? What is that there? What is air?	To encourage interest and curiosity. To encourage own questions and explanations.	Difficult for children to manipulate, however, practice made perfect! Adult presence needed.	S–watched, didn't touch. J–very excited, lot of movement to express excitement, but couldn't express self except through movement. Jo–explained it must be air – in answer to what is air – 'air is air, we breathe it'.	Get book for Jo, actually bring S and J to water tray tomorrow. Limit number of children. Write out some questions on cards to read.
Creative–junk, tape, scissors, writing materials, extra things – twigs, leaves, pipe cleaners, piece of coloured cardboard – large and small, sweet wrappers.			Used continuously, 12 children.	P–created advent calendar, took 20 minutes of uninterrupted concentration, shared at group time, although hadn't shown creation to anyone – very self contained – see his notes for detail. D, G, A and H–had difficulty with scissors.	Set up cutting activity, maybe just cutting paper for creative table, for D, G, A and H, all week.

Table 2.4 *continued*

Area/Activity include Resources/Equipment	Possible questions, explanations	Learning intentions/ areas of learning	Who used area and how, including extra equipment brought in	Learning, under-standing, and talk	Next steps, in terms of provision/resource and children's learning
Book Corner outside – tape recorders with 7 stories read from our collection, plus ruck-sacks for use outside or in, with equipment from the various stories.	Why, how, who, where, what questions. Plus statements – I expect, I would hope, maybe this is going to happen, what do you think? Shall you/ we pretend we are...? Surprised, "Look at this, there is a rucksack here with . . . in? How strange."	To develop link between picture book and storying. To encourage R, F, J, N, W, G, P, to story and play and enjoy picture books. To encourage anticipation in story.			
Construction Area		See medium term plans.	F, J, M, C, A, Ap as a group, brought in wallpaper, trucks, furniture.	F just moved house – lots of acting out the scene, noise, bustle, activity.	Set up as left today – to continue play. Discuss group time, songs re subject – "here we go round the removal van."

Source: University of Reading, PGCE Primary Programme.

Figure 2.2
Parent and staff member greeting first thing in the morning.

Setting up and tidying away

Having a good outdoor area inevitably means there will be more work for the staff members to do. However, it is possible to cut the workload by not spending hours setting up for the children, creating a ready-made environment with worn out adults! The fashion of setting up every area with the Leaning Tower of Pisa from Lego, Rome created in wooden blocks and the Fiat bike made out of tissue paper seems to strike me as a complete waste of time. If we return to the discussion about dispositions for learning, then beautiful creations by the adult will not allow children to experiment, show initiative or be creative. An educational space, whether in or out, needs to have resources and equipment available, and, most importantly, an ethos that says 'anything is possible'.

So the equipment needs to be stored in such a way that is safe for children to access and labelled clearly so they know what is where and where to put things away. The shed should not be full of 26 bikes/tricycles. The shed should be shelved and labelled and the equipment and resources arranged logically so they are completely accessible to children. DIY stores produce sheds of various sizes and shapes that can be used to house an imaginative scene: a street café or a railway station, or for the housing of construction equipment or blocks. All the adult or child needs to do is unlock the padlock and bring out housed equipment such as the café chairs and table. In these ways, setting up can become much less time consuming, and children can access resources as they wish in a workshop environment. Also, children learn to be independent and responsible, and staff members are saved an inordinate amount of time not

Figures 2.3a–2.3b
To ensure children can use and tidy away, make sure the resources are accessible and organised, as are these brooms and spades.

Figure 2.3c
These children are keen to ensure these bricks fit properly into this container, collecting and arranging together. All children, boys and girls, should tidy up.

having to lug things everywhere. Use tarpaulin to cover equipment once the day is done. This can either be nailed in place (for example, a woodwork table against a wall could have wooden battens with tarpaulin attached to the wall, which can then be pulled over the table at the end of the day to keep it from the weather). Or tarpaulin can be thrown over equipment and held down with bricks. If you are not able to have fixed storage sheds, then boxes and trolleys that are moved into the outdoor space from inside are a solution. But children should still be able to make choices for themselves about what they want to use in their work and experimentation.

Of course, at times, it is appropriate to set up the equipment as it gives starting points to children, who may be unsure as to what they can do or want to do. Therefore, sometimes we can set up an interesting arrangement of equipment or a collection of resources that can be the key to starting the play. Likewise, photographs can offer starting points for children. Make sure you always have a number of small photograph albums with images of children playing with the various pieces of equipment and resources. Small, inexpensive rucksacks filled with items can also be a great starting point for play. You can fill them with anything! For example, a wind-up torch, Post-it notes, pencils, a map and a hat could be the start of some very inventive play. The same materials can be put back for the play to continue the next day. Children can also fill their own rucksacks to start an adventure. Do not forget, the mere presence of an adult can start the play.

In terms of tidying away, all children must be involved; it is not fair to allow some to get away with being lazy. Tidying up should happen as the day goes on. An area can become used and needs to be tidied so other children can use the equipment. But at the end of the day, there also needs to be a general tidy up, just as at the end of the half terms and terms there should be a very good sort out, clean, repair and tidy session. This means tidy up time has to be well planned and orchestrated. You need to set aside a chunk of time for tidying and view it as an opportunity for learning and developing; it has to be seen as a part of the timetabled day (see Figure 2.3c). It is indeed this if managed correctly. It means there has to be an ethos of caring and sharing so all children appreciate the relevance of what they are doing. The adults should not be viewed as the children's slaves. Once these attitudes have been instilled, children need to be taught how to manoeuvre equipment, how to carry, stack, arrange, fold and so on. Children can be assigned tasks; some can even be given the role of inspector! With a clipboard, pencil and list of areas to be checked, they can take responsibility for deciding whether an area meets their standards. It takes effort to organise tidy up time well and fairly; done badly, it encourages deception, unkindness and often sexism.

Playing and working with children

Children do need time to play purposefully without adults; they need a level of freedom to work things out for themselves and between themselves. At these times, the adult needs to be in an 'at hand' role, so that possible problems can be averted (for example, slippery shoes on the metal climbing apparatus). However, children need to know that when they need an adult, they can access one, as though the adult were a resource. Adults will also have specific children they wish to work with, and they can take advantage of those incidental times during play to do this.

There are good reasons for joining in with children's play:

- learning increases;

- the quality of play and conversation improves;

- the status of the play and activity is raised;

Figure 2.4a–2.4c
These adults are joining in with the play. The adult is talking to the child about her drawings. Sometimes, it is just fun capturing the adult and making them the prisoner! It is also much easier for an adult to be in this position. Some children can be very frightened. The truck is heavy and the children do not necessarily naturally work together; the adult involvement means all is well.

- the self-esteem of those involved is raised;

- unsure children can be supported; and

- stereotypical play can be reduced.

However, being part of children's play is probably the most difficult job we do. We have to be spontaneous with ideas to ensure play does not die, mind readers to work out whether a child wants us involved or not, and full of energy to keep going (see Figures 2.4a–c).

Fine tuning

According to McLean (1991), not only do adults need to work with and alongside children, but they also need to keep a watchful eye on all that is going on to ensure the environment works effectively for all. She terms this 'fine tuning'. Staff members need to:

- manage the time and space;

- add to a play situation;

- give ideas;

- add resources;

- make sure the play of one group does not encroach on another;

- pre-empt problems;

- encourage children to try out new skills and ideas;

- stop children giving up;

- make connections for children;

- ensure children have choices; and

- make sure the space does not become too messy, and therefore useless.

Teaching

Any educational setting is about both teaching and learning, and providing and creating an environment for both to happen. Neither should be seen as more important than the other; children learning in an environment set up by you cannot be seen as secondary to learning that happens when explicit and overt teaching is happening. Otherwise, you simply undermine the whole concept of children learning alone and with other children. So children need time away from adults, but they also need input, which enables them to think and develop. Overt teaching could be where one is helping a child to improve physically (for example, catching a ball, using scissors, holding a pencil, using a bat). You do not learn these skills by chance. You have to be taught to bring your hands into your body and together to catch a ball. You need to be taught that scissors have to be held at a certain angle to work and as an extension to the hand. I have seen children struggling with cutting, with their hand facing their body – incredulous that no one has thought to correct this. Children need to be taught to 'watch the ball' when learning to use a bat, otherwise they can watch the bat, which will not lead to success. This overt skill of teaching is needed just as much as children need explicit teaching when learning the sounds of words. Children learn as they play alone and with other children, and this can only happen when the environment has been set up in the following way:

Figures 2.5–2.6

This child is being shown (taught) what being the leader is all about. Young children need to do to find out, not necessarily be told. The child on the bar has both an adult there 'just in case', but also to direct and advise about the best way to move.

- so there is equality of opportunity;

- when all children are able to access all activities;

- when all children can collect resources themselves;

- where there is a culture that celebrates success and views mistakes as an opportunity for learning, not to be ridiculed;

- where adults see their role as being a resource for children (see Figures 2.5 and 2.6); and

- where children have sufficient time and space to follow their interests.

Opportunity

Part of the adult role is to be a facilitator, to make sure it happens. Always watching to ensure there are no missed opportunities. You almost need to be part of the furniture so children hardly notice you, but then when you see a need, you can just step right in and help. Figures 2.7a and 2.7b are very different examples of the adult ensuring the opportunity is not lost. In Figure 2.7a, the children need to develop their play and just need the involvement of the adult to put an idea forward and help move the tray to continue the play. Figure 2.7b shows young children wanting to get closer to the chickens but being a little reticent; but with the adult aware of that and present to help, the children felt confident to be in the chicken pen.

> ### Case study
>
> Boys were misusing milk crates, throwing them about and so on. Rather than point the finger at the children, the staff decided to see if it was the fault of what equipment was available and how it was being provided. So they put netting over the milk crates, added Action Man dolls and Lego base plates, and the play was transformed. Children played intensive action adventures, involving lots of talk, negotiation and humour.

Challenge through conversation

By asking challenging questions or posing challenging situations, adults will enable children to really think. A challenge for one child may not be for another; you need to know your children to really offer true challenge. Challenge involves talking to and listening to children. In a recent small-scale study, the dialogues between staff and children (that is, the types of exchange that occurred when either the child approached an adult or the adult approached a child) were collated and analysed. Adults spoke more than children and the majority of interactions instigated by the adult were administrative and practical in their nature, to do with following an adult's request: 'Can you . . .', 'Don't do that . . .', 'What is . . .', rather than questions that would encourage learning. 'The results may indicate that adults are in a controlling regulatory role rather than one which is designed to facilitate language development' (Bilton 2012: 417). When the child initiated the conversation, there were more extended child utterances than domestic utterances. This suggested that children wished to be involved in conversations of depth and

Figure 2.7a
Being there to give reassurance.

Figure 2.7b
Noticing a need and helping.

Figure 2.8
This adult is interested and is talking through ideas with this child. The child is in no hurry to leave; he is also interested, and therefore motivated. The adult's body language is open and friendly.

meaning. For quality conversation to occur, quality meaning learning, there needs to be the following:

- children asking questions;
- the dialogue being about current interests or happenings (see Figure 2.8);
- the conversations often being quite lengthy;
- the adult demonstrating genuine interest in the content of the conversation (see Figure 2.12a);
- the learning occurring without direct teaching; and
- not involving the standard teacher/child interrogatory question/answer dialogue.

For this to happen, staff members need to really consider the language they wish to develop rather than simply putting the dinosaurs in the sand because a box needs to be completed on a planning sheet. There is a very strong link between talking and thinking. Enabling and planning for children to talk and have conversations that involve intellectual search need to happen all the time.

Stimulation

Children need to be interested in what they are doing, and need a reason for doing it; stimulation increases motivation, motivation increases perseverance and perseverance increases the likelihood of understanding. But more than this, there is now starting to be an agreement that intrinsic motivation (that is, motivation that comes from within) is far more important in a child's success than extrinsic motivation. We seem to be in a time when children are given, and seemingly expect, extrinsic rewards. The growing evidence is that a child needs to want to do something for him or herself for it to be successful. Extrinsic motivation actually is negatively related to attainment. This links closely to the dispositions discussed earlier on. So what does this mean for us working in the outdoor environment? Most children are pretty motivated to go out, but they need to find stimulating things to do out there for it to be worthwhile for them and for them to continue to be motivated intrinsically. A bike will often be seen as an extrinsic motivation for going out. Children will go out only to get the reward of the bike/tricycle, and some can find it almost impossible to do anything else if the bike is not there. This militates against learning or attainment, so we need to create an environment that raises the curiosity. So why does the water flow from the tube upwards? Why won't this block balance on that block, and how can I make it? How does that worm move? To create this level of stimulation, we need to be interested in and knowledgeable of the world around us.

Progression

To help children and to teach them, we need to know where we are going with them and what it is we are expecting by the time they leave us. Mathematical and linguistic development is fairly well known; there is an order and progression and knowledge about skills to be learned. However, I am not sure the same applies to other areas (for example, physical or creative development). Below is a list of motor skills children need to attain (Gallahue and Donnelly 2003: 54):

- **Locomotor development** or gross motor is about moving through the environment, which involves large movement patterns, such as: *walking, running, jumping, hopping, skipping, sliding, leaping, climbing, crawling, standing, sitting.*

- **Non-locomotor development** or stabilising maintaining equilibrium is about balancing, such as: *bending, stretching, twisting, pivoting, swinging, rolling, landing, stopping, dodging, balancing, inverted supports (upside down).*

- Manipulative or **fine motor skills** and **hand–eye** and **foot–eye coordination skills** is about imparting force on objects, such as: *throwing, catching, kicking, trapping, striking, volleying, bouncing, rolling, pulling, pushing, punting, grasping, reaching, gripping, holding (including the skills of sewing, cutting, typing, writing, drawing, painting).*

However, for each motor skill, the list of permutations is large. For example, throwing – one can throw hard or soft, high or low, under or over arm, while running, from a horizontal position, backwards or forwards, throw and bounce. For jumping, there is jumping from side to side, backwards, forwards, on the spot, down, up, across, using one foot, using two feet together, from a squat position, into or from something moving. Do we seriously take into consideration the huge number of permutations to one motor skill and thereby teach all the skills? I am not expecting all 5 year olds to dive, catch a ball and throw it to someone else accurately. However, I would expect that we would be teaching children the whole range of physical skills so that they are overall very able when they leave us.

Figure 2.9a
This adult is doing a number of very important things. She is an interested adult. She has probably seen in excess of 20,000 tadpoles, but that does not matter. This one right here, right now is the one those children are interested in! She is knowledgeable and curious, and this helps children to view these as attainable and worthwhile attributes. And so they, likewise, are interested, motivated and curious.

Figure 2.9b
This adult is supporting the children in their efforts to identify a 'minibeast'. Having the right resources to hand is critical to ensure learning progresses.

Figure 2.9c
Sometimes, children are unsure as to how to use a piece of equipment. One of the adult's roles is to demonstrate.

Figure 2.10
If we want to make quick observational notes about children, it helps if we do not have to leave them to find pen and paper. Here, the pads are hung up under the canopy.

Observation

Linked very well to teaching is observation. The trick with observation is to know what one is looking for! If the outdoor environment is set up for teaching and learning as opposed to a free-for-all, then it should be simple to make observations about the children. One way to achieve success is to be systematic. Choose a set number of children to watch every week, say four, and everyone makes a concerted effort to make much more detailed and varied observations of these particular children. Pay attention to development, but also involve them in the study of themselves, through enabling them to contribute to their learning journey and including their parents in this quite formal procedure. In a class of 30, it will take eight weeks to get through all children; basically, this is the whole class every half term. If you have a larger cohort of children or large units, then the number will have to be increased. This is not ideal, but pragmatic. But what cannot happen is that children are observed inside, but outside only taken note of half-heartedly (see Figure 2.10). If you are not completely systematic, then you will not make these long observations and are unlikely to get to know the individuals very well. And that is the point – the 'very well' bit. We need to know our children inside out to seriously help them.

Figure 2.11
The adult is 'on the ground' with the children, aware of all that is going on (not drinking a cup of tea and ignoring them), and so is able to discuss the properties of sand, but then able to point out the word, quite naturally linking action and the written word.

Adult rota

It is preferable to have as flexible a rota as possible so that staff members are not outside for the whole session; otherwise, it can end up with staff members wilting on a hot day or freezing on a cold day. If the two areas are planned and viewed as one, then it would make sense to approach the deployment of staff members in this way. Some days, there are more children in one space than another, needing more staff, so again a flexible rota ensures children can be supported well. Likewise, you may find a group of children an adult is working with want to go inside to continue some aspect of play, and they need the adult to be with them. With a flexible rota, another member of staff can swap and go outside while that staff member continues to work with his or her group inside.

'Safeness'

I have called this section 'safeness' as I feel it describes more clearly than 'safety' what a safe environment is. Safety can often be seen as a rather narrow term and in a negative light. Physically, the area has to be safe, and not dangerous or hazardous, but not without risk and challenge. Stephenson (2003) argues that risk to a 4 year old is about attempting something new, feeling on the borderline of 'out of control' (often involving height and speed) and overcoming fear. She further argues that if you make an environment hazard-free, it becomes challenge-free, and then 'children have less experience in making decisions on their own, less opportunity to assess their own personal frontiers and less opportunity to gain confidence and self-esteem through coping independently' (Stephenson 2003: 42). While we need to be aware of the negative effects of risk, we also need to focus on the positive effects, such as raised confidence, bravery, strength and success. If we make an environment completely risk-free, we will make children less safe. All of us feel a sense of achievement if we complete something that, for us, feels risky. But 'safeness' is more than just about height and speed; it can also cover anything a child may feel is risky, and, for some, this could be putting pen to paper, so we have to make sure children feel safe to have a go at anything. 'Safeness' is about enabling things to happen, not shutting down opportunities. In case you are thinking of blaming the Health and Safety Executive (HSE) for stopping everything, have a laugh and go to the HSE website and read their myth busters page. For example:

> Issue: A press story is saying that health and safety is the barrier to children enjoying everyday activities such as playing conkers, using skipping ropes or climbing trees. Panel decision: Skipping, playing conkers and football and climbing trees are all important activities which help children to have fun and learn about handling risk at the same time. There is no health and safety legislation which bans these activities in fact HSE is on record as encouraging schools to allow these activities to go ahead. If individual schools choose to ban these activities it is for other reasons not health and safety.

> (HSE 2012)

Figure 2.12a
Here, the adult is fully involved and interested in the child.

Figure 2.12b
Children putting on their wellington boots. The conversation was about sizes: 'Our shoes are the same', 'What about that size?', 'What number is it?', 'Those are the same'. These conversations came from the simple exercise of putting the right boots on, which had been arranged carefully with each pair having its correct size painted clearly on the bottom.

Often, when health and safety are suggested as a reason not to do something, it is not true; it is just others using prevent and obstruct as they are frightened. To make a safe environment, think about the following:

- Be aware of dangers and hazards in the setting and get rid of these problems.

- Make a risk assessment of the outdoor area and check this regularly.

- But, very importantly, make sure there is challenge for all children.

- Decide what clothing and footwear you feel is suitable for outside (see Figure 2.12b).

- Discuss regularly with children 'safeness', risk and challenge.

- Write a 'safeness' policy that can be passed on to the parents and carers.

- Make sure the area is safe for all children to have a go at any activity.

- When outside, staff members need to be ever watchful, even if they are engrossed in an activity with a particular group of children.

Figures 2.13a–2.13c
Children playing with lightsabres; no one is getting hurt or having their own play disturbed.

Play fighting and real fighting

There is play fighting, sometimes referred to as rough and tumble, and there is real fighting, known as aggression, and they are different. Children need to learn to play fight and understand the difference between that and real fighting (see Figures 2.13a–c). Often, popular children get to know the difference, and less popular children do not (Pellegrini 1988). The role of the adult is to allow play fighting, but intercept when there is any danger of it moving to real aggression, to identify those children who need help in knowing the difference. Blurton-Jones (1967: 355) identified seven movement patterns associated with play fighting:

1   running;

2   chasing and felling;

3   wrestling;

4   jumping up and down with both feet together;

5   beating at each other with an open hand without actually hitting;

6   beating at each other with an object but not hitting;

7   laughing; and

8   sometimes falling and throwing body to the ground.

We cannot allow our own prejudices or lack of understanding to stop children play fighting. From it, they learn to read people and their intentions, to decentre and to find out what it is like to be victim and aggressor. By identifying those children who seem unaware of the difference between play and real fighting, we can identify those who may have problematic backgrounds that we need to address. Holland's (2003) fascinating study of gun play endorses this view that children need to be allowed to fight, make guns and incorporate this into their play. To not do this causes greater problems for both girls and boys.

Questions

- Look at your practice. Is any stereotypical behaviour going on? What is causing it? Can you change the environment to stop this behaviour?

- We are all guilty of assuming that how we should do something is how we actually do it and that the plans match what we actually do in practice, but this is often not the case! Are *all* the adults in the setting working with *all* the children and working at *all* the activities?

- Do you ever recreate a play scene from the day before? Could you think about doing this, thereby extending the play?

- Are observations of children outside shared with parents in the same way as activities inside?

- Can adults get involved in play that enables the children to take control and take the lead?

3 The curriculum out of doors

In this chapter, I will be looking at how to offer the whole curriculum in the outdoor area.

The curriculum has to be arranged both across time and across the space. We may cut the time across a day into chunks devoted to a particularly aspect(s) of the curriculum – so, for example, literacy from 9.00 a.m. to 9.20 a.m. But we also offer the curriculum across the space, so at any one time we may have a number of activities available (for example, role play, graphics, technology, small motor skill activities, etc.), and therefore aspects of the curriculum. These areas are usually referred to as zones, or areas, or bays, or experiences. Zones may cover specific curriculum areas, such as music in a music corner, or many, as a role-play area will; this may cover personal and social aspects of the curriculum, languages because of the amount of speaking and listening, or science because the role play could be a building site. The space as a whole has to ensure it is covering as many areas of the curriculum as possible. The most useful description of the areas of learning, I feel, is still that listed by the DES (1989), namely:

- linguistic and literary;
- aesthetic and creative;
- human and social;
- mathematical;
- moral;
- physical;
- scientific;
- technological; and
- spiritual.

For ease of understanding, I coined the phrase 'learning bays' and considered that the following bays were essential to provide in the outdoor environment:

- imaginative play;
- building, construction and material play;
- gross motor development;
- fine motor development;
- gardening/horticulture;
- environmental and scientific discovery;
- creative development, including drawing, art and music; and
- quiet reflection.

In totality, these bays, if set up correctly, will cover all areas of the curriculum together. But how these are provided will depend on the needs of the children in the class and school, and the layout of the environment. What has saddened me since the coining of the 'learning bay' phrase in 1998 is that some settings have considered it necessary to simply fill the outdoor space so it is as cluttered as inside. This was not my intention when I created the phrase. So a plea to everyone is 'please do not fill the outside space'; allow for space and freedom for children to do as they wish in that space.

It may be worth remembering that Tovey (2007) talks in terms of both creating a space and a place outside. A useful analogy is what we do with where we live. We live in houses – the space – but we make them into homes – the place. Each garden must make sure they turn their space into a special place and each will be different, just as each home is different to the next. Figure 3.1 feels like a place, rather than just a space. The nursery school has a large tree that has been made more of by being incorporated into a play area. It feels like a special place, felt by adults and children.

Likewise, Walsh (1991) talks in terms of creating open, active and quiet areas within a garden. Again, these are useful divisions, and structure one's thinking so that the full curriculum is considered. The open space would be a flexible space for the freedom of movement, involving, say, moveable equipment. There could be flat areas, but also mounds, and three-dimensional effects. The active area is where children will need to be just that: physically active say digging or climbing. The quiet area involves more sedentary approach, and could include a sandpit, more formal adult and child activities, a child's garden and secret places. Another way of considering the area is to look at Edgington (2003). She has the following suggestions for an outside area:

- a climbing area;
- space to run;
- a wheeled-vehicle area;
- space to develop skills with small equipment;
- a quiet area;
- places to hide;
- a wild area;
- an area for large-scale construction and imaginative play;
- space for play with natural material; and
- a gardening area.

Or you could divide it by the ways children work and play, which are:

- imaginative play;
- design and construction;
- communication and language; and
- investigation and exploration.

Figure 3.1a
This is an example of making the most of a natural resource in a garden. This school is lucky and does have a large tree but they have chosen to make a feature of it and so zone a space for imaginative play and games.

Whatever way you structure the area, you may like to think about the following:

- If you list actual equipment (for example, 'climbing frame, house, monkey bars'), you may find that you see each piece of equipment as only being able to provide for one curriculum area, whereas the climbing frame could be used as a den or as a scaffold to hold equipment for a science experiment.

- In the same way, if you zone space into how children work and play (as above), then equipment does not have to be static; sand could be used in the investigative area or it could be used in the imaginative area.

- Under each zone would come a variety of activities to fit the description. So, for example, under 'designing and making', one would include technology, woodwork and painting.

- Think about what you want children to do when they use the various areas outside. We want children to think, imagine, design, construct, make, communicate, investigate, explore and move. These descriptions are wide (for example, 'communicate' could be verbally, through drawings, writings, dance and/or music). Under 'imagine', we would want children to be creative, to invent and to be original. Thinking involves the ability to consider, ponder, deliberate, reflect and make judgements.

- Make sure children have plenty of opportunities to set up and run their own ideas.

- Make sure all areas or zones accommodate children playing together and alone.

On the following pages are the zones I suggest, with resources, ideas and *aides-memoires*.

Imaginative play

Resources

- A-frames
- planks – commercially made and cut to order by a DIY store
- ladders
- cubes
- heavy pieces of material
- plastic sheeting/tarpaulin
- wheeled toys – trucks, pushchairs, prams, carts, wheelbarrows
- plastic crates – bread, milk, supermarket
- blocks – wooden and plastic
- large cardboard boxes
- industrial tubing
- cable spools (a variety of sizes up to 1 metre in diameter)
- tree trunk sections
- pieces of carpet and carpet squares
- tents
- large cones
- broom handles – a broom handle dropped into a large can, or parasol base filled with sand or set in a tub of cement, can be used to attach a sign to, or to drape material over to form a den or sun shade, or to attach a washing line between two
- hose pipe – cut to lengths for fire-fighting equipment and for sand and water play
- imaginative props (for example, a collection of props around a particular occupation)
- clothes, including a huge selection of bags and hats
- holiday equipment – backpacks, sleeping bags, cooking stuff, suitcases, picnic bags
- builder's tools and equipment – mallets, screwdrivers, spirit levels, pulleys
- DIY tools and tool belts, paintbrushes, pulleys
- mechanic tools
- large umbrellas
- decorator's tools – brushes, pots
- ropes and pegs – the rope is a most versatile resource (for example, it can be used for skipping, to attach a truck to a bike, made into a letter or number shape, formed into a circle to jump in and out of, laid out for balancing along and, with a label attached to it, can become a petrol pump)
- gardening tools – shovels, spades, watering cans, sweeping brushes, pots
- home tools – cameras, mobile phones, personal stereos, binoculars, umbrellas, money, purses, tickets, cards
- fire-fighting equipment
- doctor's bag and equipment, home-made stretcher
- fishing rods, maps, sunglasses, jewellery

Ideas

- garden centre
- boat
- pirate ship
- post office (think eBay and Amazon)
- sorting office
- pizza delivery and pizza shop
- supermarket delivery depot and shop
- flower delivery
- builder/plasterer
- removal firm
- beauty parlour
- launderette
- organised sport/dance event
- dinosaur land
- removals
- TV repair and reception
- fairy-tale castle
- garage reception and repairs
- fire station and fire engine
- ice cream seller
- library
- dispatch rider
- artist
- inventors
- school
- soldiers/police
- mountaineering
- planes and flying

Remember

- Link imaginative play scenes inside and out.
- You do not have to set these areas up, but you do need to have the ideas and ability to facilitate the play.
- Inspire children by reading stories and providing relevant props.
- Outdoors allows movement and play on a large scale.
- The resources are almost endless.
- Do involve the children in the choice and design of focused imaginative areas.
- Provide many imaginative areas. In real life, we move from one situation to another, whether it be from the home to the shops, to work, to the library and so on; children need the same opportunities.
- Do provide imaginative play every day.
- Make sure children are able to set up their own imaginative games too.

Figures 3.1b–3.1d

These two children were immersed and absorbed in a game of getting 'two tickets and a tack'. They spent much of an hour running back and forth and running at speed. If one glanced at them, it would appear they were not spending their time wisely, just 'running about'.

But I was in a position just to watch. What they were actually saying was difficult to catch, but I think they were talking about tickets and tacks. I could not understand the second word; it could have been 'attack'.

One boy was far more confident than the other and willing to venture out from the protection of the tree; this was clearly the den/hideout.

The other boy was more reticent in venturing out to get the 'two tickets and a tack'. He needed a lot of encouragement and cajoling.

They were in a completely other world, unaware of anyone in the garden. They were in an imaginary game and it was, at times, scary.

The space, the time, the lack of interruption, the safety of that nursery garden gave them the security to play that game.

What were they learning? To run, swerve, anticipate, imagine, plan, discuss, support each other and cooperate.

They were also feeling on the border of out of control (see page 34).

Case study

One school liked to discuss with the children what imaginative areas they would like. On this occasion, the children wanted a removals firm. Initially, the staff members found books and information on the subject, encouraging the families to do likewise. Children do not necessarily know a great deal about a particular occupation, and so staff members role-played typical removal scenes. For about a week, there were discussions about the subject of moving house, storing furniture, the reasons for moving, distances travelled and so on. A variety of empty boxes were collected, plus a host of household items, and two houses were set up, one inside and one outside, and so the removals started. Pull-along trunks had roofs attached using broom handles and a large piece of material. Each day, the play was assessed, resources added and new activities set up. A real removal man came into the setting and talked to the children, and his funny stories were then used in their play! Significant from the play was the high level of negotiating skills (around furniture getting stuck and how furniture would fit together in a truck) and the improvement in spatial awareness; all this with lots of laughter.

Building, construction and material play

Resources

- A-frames
- planks
- cubes
- crates
- ladders
- different sized cardboard boxes
- cable spools (a variety of sizes up to 1 metre in diameter)
- plastic tubing, guttering, hosepipes
- any wooden blocks – non-standard, unit and hollow logs and tree branches of various sizes and lengths
- sanded wooden offcuts
- breeze blocks
- bricks

Materials

- funnels
- a variety of containers, jugs and digging implements, including spades with strong shafts
- DIY builders trays or large trays from stores such as IKEA
- collections of: stones, shells, twigs, pebbles, bark, cork, leaves, gravel, sea glass, cones, beads, wool, feathers, string
- ropes

Figures 3.2a–3.2h

Every early-years setting should have these Community Plaything blocks. They are the most versatile, adaptable, solid, hard-wearing resources possible, and the possibilities for teaching and learning are endless. Here, these blocks are positioned outside underneath the canopy. I was not aware of this child's schema, but he set to with the equipment and played for over 20 minutes. Note the concentration, the consideration, the creation. He was designing considering the aesthetics and also designing for purpose – a slope to run a cylinder down.

Ideas

- Transporting – children of this age like to and gain a great deal from transporting materials, such as pebbles, twigs, etc. So ensure you have plenty of transporting vehicles such as wheelbarrows.

- Building a tower using wooden offcuts and mud.

- Building a bridge using crates and planks.

- Building a den using cubes/boxes and material.

- Building a construction using crates, guttering, funnels and jugs to move water from one place to another.

- Digging a tunnel in the sand and supporting the sides with blocks, twigs and small logs.

- Making patterns with logs, stones and embroidery rings.

- Damming up the water flow, changing the course of flow using a waterspout and stones and pebbles (for example, by using a fixed water feature).

Remember

- This area could include:
  - building;
  - woodwork;
  - sand and water play, not necessarily in trays and pits; and
  - digging plot.

- This bay involves mathematical and linguistic development, including understanding of weight, density, volume, position and relationship of objects to each other. It will involve the language of negotiation, discussion, possibilities, why and if, and future ideas.

- Building and construction often leads to imaginative play.

- You do not need to replicate provision. If there is sand outside, it does not have to be inside too. Think about having two sand areas outside, so that sand can be transported, but watch for sand on hard surfaces, as it can become very slippery. Or have a small coal bunker-type shed from a DIY store and fill it with sand so that it can be scooped out and used in play. Or use a piece of material on the ground for sand.

- Give children the opportunities to work alone, as well as together, on projects.

- Keep a project ongoing by setting it up the next day in the same way as the children left it the previous day.

- Use carpet squares or thick cardboard so children can sit on the ground even when it is damp and cold.

- The digging area could include logs, stones, dinosaurs or small world figures for construction and imaginative play.

- Have hooks positioned around the outside area, so when one wants to attach or hold a rope, musical instrument, pulley or whatever, it can be done immediately.

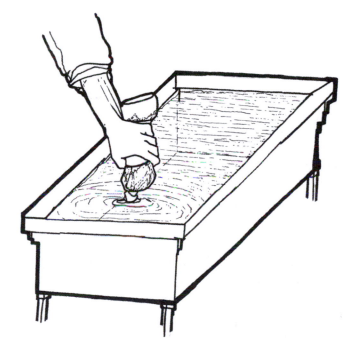

Figures 3.2i–3.2l

These images suggest how good sand and water play can be achieved. The resources to be used with the sand and water should be carefully stored and labelled; staff members need to think of the materials in terms of experiments (not as a repository for toy dinosaurs) – for example, when siphoning or learning about vacuums, staff need to get together and think about the language they might use with regard to the materials, and display these and revisit the language and ideas regularly. Look at the language ideas coming from the tap! © Josh Bilton

Gross motor development

Resources

- planks
- A-frames or nesting bridges
- moveable climbing frame
- carpet squares
- boxes
- crates
- cubes
- barrels
- tunnels
- ladders
- hoops
- half logs
- tyres
- cones
- canes
- ropes
- trees and logs – think about fundraising to buy trees to plant that, in time, will have grown large enough for climbing
- 'monkey bars' – a thick rope secured between two posts will serve as a monkey bar

Ideas

- Challenge children to move around the equipment without touching the ground.
- Challenge children to move quickly, yet deliberately, like a particular animal.
- Challenge children to think of as many ways as they can to get around the equipment.
- Ask children to follow a sequence of letters or numbers.
- Link up a number of gymnasium layouts.
- Ask children to set up the equipment so they stay as close to the ground as possible.

Remember

- Obstacle courses are for children to work on alone or with friends, not in competition with each other.
- Allow children to set up the arrangement of equipment themselves.
- This bay is about developing physical activity and physical skills – agility, balance, coordination and strength.
- Children need plenty of opportunities to practise, modify and refine their movements in order to reach a mature pattern of movement and a high level of self-confidence.
- Adults need to offer guidance, support and encouragement.
- Adults need to be aware of what skills they are hoping children will gain and not expect children to 'catch' the learning.
- Allow children to feel a sense of achievement by being able to take risks, try something new and/or overcome fear.
- Appreciate and acknowledge what children are learning and can do.

Case study

The children and one member of staff talked about having an Olympics-style/athletics track arrangement of equipment outside. Some children clearly had more idea of the concepts than others, but the teacher had already created a montage of images and words for the computer for the children to watch and listen to. A number of children arranged resources, such as a rope and piece of material for the long jump, cane and stands for high jump, balls in a hoop for a throwing game, rope laid on the ground for tightrope and so on. The older children were keen to organise everything and to give out instructions, the younger children were keen to organise their own space. The fluidity of the activity and the amount of space meant all could follow their own learning journey. At different levels of involvement children partook of the 'games'. The degree of cooperation and the similarity of interest between boys and girls was significant, as was the extent to which children used the language of negotiation.

Fine motor development

Resources

- balls – various sizes, weights and materials
- ropes – with and without ends
- bats – various long and short handled, make sure they are not too heavy
- hoops – various sizes
- bean bags (except in the wet, as they get very heavy)
- baskets and buckets to catch balls in
- stilts (see Figure 3.3)

Ideas

- Aiming at targets, into a basket.
- Hook the duck.
- Hoopla.
- Rolling, estimating and measuring.
- Set up a game – bowling, tennis, golf.

Remember

- Combine the more formal curriculum with motor-skill development. This can often encourage children who are reticent about reading and writing.
- This area can get out of hand, so think of ways of containing balls. Have a ball tied into the leg of an old pair of tights, tied to a washing line; for batting, have containers to throw balls into, tie a hoop to a washing line to throw through.
- You do not need lots of fancy and expensive equipment. Just attach an opened coat hanger to a sturdy object for a basketball net and use boxes on the ground to aim into.
- Allow children to set up their own games.

Case study

Two children were digging without much focus in the sandpit. The teacher happened to have a reference book about tunnels and bridges. She sat down by the sandpit and started to look at the book, the children became interested in what she was looking at and, without any prompting, they started to talk about the images. This soon turned to the children chatting almost separately, going off to collect resources – wheelbarrows, wooden offcuts, trowels, twigs. They then set about making a tunnel and bridge using all of the resources collected. This took over an hour, with a great deal of consideration, discussion and manipulation of materials. The important thing of note is the subtlety with which the teacher introduced the idea to the children through the book. As all the materials were recycled, the set-up was left overnight, and as the children were full-time and they did not have vandals, the arrangement was there for the children to continue working on the next day.

Figure 3.3a
Stilts can be bought or made. They form an important repertoire of materials for children to improve balance and hand-eye coordination and physical confidence. But it does involve skill teaching. This staff member was asking questions to help the child to improve his skills: 'How far can you go?', 'Can you get to me?', 'Shall I go back further?'

Case study

The teacher in a nonchalant way started to strap, using string, a piece of guttering to the climbing frame. When children asked her what she was doing, she said, 'I wanted to find out how far all the guttering we had would stretch across the garden.' Rather than saying in a rather formalised way, 'We are going to . . .', this was less formal and so the children were far more keen to be involved. Children set to and found guttering to strap to any piece of equipment for themselves, discussing and negotiating exactly where and how the guttering would be put. In the end, there was a continuous path of probably 12 metres! This creation inspired a child to start a ball run, which then led to the replacing of guttering to make it continuously downhill so the balls could roll. Balls were caught at the end and run to the beginning almost endlessly. Significant in this activity was the apparently casual approach of the teacher; the ability to use the whole space as this setting considered the outside to be a flexible area, and the way construction (science) actually led to other areas of the curriculum and development (motor skills).

Gardening/horticulture

Resources

- ground or any kind of container for growing
- child size and adult size:
  - spades
  - trowels
  - forks
  - gardening gloves
  - wheelbarrows
- watering cans
- truggs
- hose (see Figure 3.3a)
- plant plots
- canes
- seeds/plants
- water butt/outside tap – so children can collect water when they want and it can be used in any part of the outside area (see Figure 3.3a)
- camera
- writing and drawing materials

Ideas

- From September onwards, plant bulbs for a spring show; for example, daffodils, tulips and crocuses.
- In May, after the last frosts, plant the following for a summer and early autumn show: corms, bulbs and tubers (for example, anemones, freesia, iris, *Liatris spicata* and dahlias); vegetables (for example, beans, carrots, peas, marrows, potatoes (also the early variety), lettuce, cucumber and tomatoes); and annuals (for example, cosmos, marigolds and petunias); hardy annual seeds (for example, alyssum, *Asperula* species, candytuft, clarkia, clary, lavatera, *Limnanthes* species, nasturtium, scabious and Virginia stock).
- Plant evergreen zones, same-colour plant zones, aromatic zones and texture zones.
- Use the seasonal cropping as the themes for the year.

Remember

- This area is about planting, tending and harvesting, not planting, forgetting to tend and dying. Do not attempt this activity if it is not going to be seen through.

- You do not have to be an expert gardener but this area does need thoughtful planning.

- Children need to record the life cycle in words, drawings, photographs, collage, paint, computer-generated graphs and any other medium possible.

- This area is about beauty, comparison and change. It is to engender feelings of curiosity and awe.

- Plant heights can be measured, crops can be weighed, textures and smells compared, crops and petals counted, vegetables and fruit eaten!

- Make books charting the development of the plants. This is useful to encourage reading, writing and mathematical work with those children who are reticent about such things. Making labels and writing up rotas will also help with writing skills.

- This area would benefit from some form of low boundary fence or layer of bricks, so children appreciate this is a working environment and is not for play purposes.

- Children can be part of the planning process, looking forward to what jobs will need to be done next in the garden.

- Think very carefully about when the cycle will be complete, to ensure children do not leave before they have seen and tasted the fruits of their labour.

- Draw children's attention to the plants. Just because we notice things does not mean a child has done so.

Figure 3.3b
Water and hose outside.

Figure 3.3c–3.3h

Here are some examples of gardens. Raised box gardens enable everyone to use them. Young, old, those with specific movement needs. Lower boxed gardens mean the garden is contained and manageable and every spot is reachable. The strange looking pile (3.3e) is what is called a keyhole garden (www.organicgarden.org.uk/ urban-micro-farming/keyhole-gardens). This is basically a pile of compost in the middle, which is watered and the plants to be grown put in the soil piled around the central pile. This is the produce from one nursery garden – critical to the learning potential of gardening is the cropping. A garden with a fence, to delineate it from the rest of the outdoor area, with a stile as a gate. A photograph is a great way to display what will be next to what is at the moment!

Case study

In September, a setting in Norfolk planted bulbs around the outline of the tallest child. When the bulbs came through in March, children were able to lie inside the outline of bulbs and were quite enclosed by the tall leaves and stalks. They could view the sky from a horizontal position and view the plants close up.

Case study

Children were taken to a local garden centre and bought a range of bulbs, having spent quite some time discussing and looking at the plants online.

Some children were able to take a paper bag and fill the bag to the brim with a variety of bulbs for a set price!

Back at the school, the whole group discussed the project, and it was called a project, not a topic or theme. This was a growing bulbs project.

Over the course of the next few weeks (this was early September), the children discussed what they were going to do, what they were going to plant where and the tools that were needed. Drawings and plans were put together. Then the children and staff started the planting process, in small interested groups, over a two-day period.

Alongside the work was the creation of a diary/book about the project, charting each step of the way, using photographs, drawings, graphs, writing (actual and scribe), and also the construction of a timeline. This started on day one when the bulbs were planted, and each day another square was coloured in to denote that the bulbs were in situ but had not grown above the ground. When the bulb shoots started to emerge, a different colour was used to denote this change, and this was continued with a colour denoting the emergence of the first flower opening and the first flower dying.

In an extremely simple way, the children were able to view the passage of time, and to discuss and agree upon such decisions as when the flower was showing enough to mark the timeline, when the flower was showing signs of degeneration to mark the timeline. The book was then finally donated to the nursery's book corner!

This project was a good example of how a practical and useful class project, including children at a variety of levels and intensities and roles, was managed over a long period of time, incorporating a vast number of curriculum areas, and shows how a small topic can be made into a big and long-term project. We are all too often trying to find new experiences for children when what we should be doing is making more of what we are already doing.

Environmental and scientific discovery

Resources

- environments for:
  - birds (boxes (with a camera make a fantastic long-term resource), feeding tables, water baths, trees)
  - animals (wild area)
  - 'minibeasts' (tree trunk sections, old carpet, large stones, evergreen cuttings)
  - fish and amphibians (water) (see Figure 3.4e)
  - bats (boxes)
  - guinea pigs/rabbits/chickens (see Figures 3.4b–d)
- collecting pots
- magnifying glasses
- drawing and writing materials
- gathering jars, and sheets to collect insects from trees, as well as paint brushes for picking up invertebrates
- pond-dipping equipment
- nets
- weather boxes
- camera
- flip camera
- audio recorder
- Go on the RSPB website and the Woodland Trust website. There are lots of resources available, and most are free: www.rspb.org.uk/ourwork/teaching/catalogue/early_years.aspx and www.woodlandtrust.org.uk/
- wormery/compost (see Figure 3.4a)

Ideas

- A project on 'minibeasts', or insects, or invertebrates, or an aspect of the weather could start from this zone.
- A project focusing on close observational drawing.
- A project involving difference; for example, using Venn diagrams.
- Rotas needed for cleaning/feeding animals.
- Pour water on an area of grass/soil and wait for the worms to come up. Use a sand timer to see how long it takes for them to appear and then disappear.
- Weather boxes, an idea from Ouvry (2000), suggests making up boxes of collections for each weather feature, namely wind, sun, snow, rain, and also frost and fog. Into these boxes put songs, rhymes, stories, poems, photographs, pictures, taped sounds, ideas and resources for experiments. Children could add ideas, their own drawings, poems and stories. It is very important to decide what you are trying to achieve and enable children to learn before you collect the resources. So, for example, with rain, it would be about the various levels of rain, from light to heavy, the channels rain will take once it is on the ground, the quantity of rain, the study of clouds and the effect of rain. Equally, it needs to be about enjoying rain and being able to be in it while being protected from it. You can also create weather features to experiment with.
- Setting up a camera bird box.

Remember

- This area does not have to take up a great deal of space.
- With the children, make books or laminated cards that specifically identify the organisms in their garden.
- This is an area about valuing the organisms in our area, not grown-ups being frightened of worms.
- One has to be knowledgeable and be able to point out the difference between, for example, a centipede and a millipede.
- Make children aware of what is around; children can only notice and behave amazed if they are taught to.
- This will involve both informal discoveries and actual planned projects.
- Try out the weather experiments on the Met Office website: www.metoffice.gov.uk/education/kids/things-to-do/experiments.

Figure 3.4a

A compost but also a wormery! The card reads, 'We put food waste from lunch club and snack times into the wormery. The worms turn it into compost that is really good for growing plants in the allotment.'

Case study

Keep resources and lists of ideas, books to read and refer to and songs to sing ready for the particular weather feature, such as rain, sun, fog, snow or wind.

A snowy day box

- Use salt to sprinkle on the ice and see what happens. Use other powdery substances and see what happens.
- Get a cup full of snow and see how the size/volume changes once it melts.
- Get a transparent container with some water in it and ice cubes so it is full to the top. Ask the children what will happen when the ice cubes melt.
- Fill a beaker with snow and take its temperature. Then, after two hours, take its temperature again. Use a thermometer probe linked to a computer to measure the temperature.
- Put one ice cube on a flat surface, see how big the puddle is when it melts and mark the outer perimeter. Then put another ice cube on the surface and predict how wide and deep the puddle will be.
- Put a drop of food colouring on the top of the ice cube and see what happens.
- Freeze different coloured ice cubes, put them on kitchen towel and ask the children to predict which will melt the fastest.

Making frost

- First, fill an empty can (soup can, coffee can, etc.) two-thirds full with crushed ice. Spread about a teaspoon full of water on a piece of paper. Place underneath the can.
- Next, fill the remainder of the can with salt and mix it with the ice. Keep mixing for a few minutes or until well mixed. Frost will start to appear on the outside of the can.
- Freeze water in boxes with lids on, and the expansion causes the lids to pop off. Keep checking the freezer!
- Experiments to do with melting: www.parentingscience.com/preschool-science-experiment.html.

Don't forget to have books in the box for snowy days:

- *Percy the Park Keeper* series and *One Snowy Night* by Nick Butterworth
- *Kipper's Snowy Day* by Mick Inkpen
- *The Snowman* by Raymond Biggs
- *Jolly Snow* by Jane Hissey
- *First Snow* by Kim Lewis
- *The Snow Queen* by H. C. Anderson
- *Penguins in the Fridge* by Nicola Moon and Peter Day

Figures 3.4b–3.4d

This school finds that care for animals has multiple benefits. For children who are settling it helps them to feel useful and gives them a sense of importance. Children learn to feed and clean the animals, to be careful when touching and to watch calmly. Staff and children naturally chat and this supports oral language development.

Figure 3.4e
A pond can be easily made. It does not need to be huge to be effective. This is raised, so it is very accessible to all.

Creative development

Resources

- charcoal
- pastels
- oil paints
- clay
- chalks
- boards to lean on
- board for oil painting
- paper (thick and thin)
- sand
- natural materials
- glue

Ideas

- Group painting – that is, painting together at the same time, for example using a very large round piece of paper divided into, say, eight sections, each eighth to be used by one child. It sounds strange but works very well!
- Large or small pieces of paper taped to the ground or to the fence.
- Foot printing and hand printing.
- Drawing constructions, flowers, scenes in the garden.
- An art project using ice (www.artfulparent.com/2012/07/melting-ice-science-experiment-with-salt-liquid-watercolors.html). No worries about mess.
- Observational drawings of specific plants that the setting has grown.
- Clay using no tools – how many ways can it be touched (poked, thumped, stroked, clawed, squashed, rolled, etc.)?
- Sand and water sculptures.
- Art ephemera, either on the ground or using the fence to weave and attach.
- Make bookmarks using double-sided Sellotape on thin card to stick flowers, leaves, etc.
- Create permanent art outside.

Remember

- Drawing is about communicating and making sense of ideas and feelings. Matthews (2003) argues how all-encompassing drawing is linking thinking, movement and feelings. Make sure children have constant access to drawing materials, whether it be chalking on the ground or drawing on a piece of cardboard or paper. Value drawing by remembering it is as important as writing.
- All famous artists have created pictures outside.
- Outside gives a different light and shadow to inside.
- Outside mess does not matter as much as inside – so use the more messy resources, such as charcoal, outside.
- Outside is a far better place to do an observational picture because it provides a greater level of inspiration.
- Art is about me, not about someone else's ideas.
- Add seeds from the pet shop and feathers (baked in the oven to kill germs) for art ephemera.
- Dark corners outside can create very good reflections.

Case study

Gary did not like mess, on his body or clothes, and he avoided dough, clay, paint and mud, and so his involvement with art materials was quite limited. One day, foot printing was offered outside. Gary watched and eventually took his shoes and socks off and did indeed do some foot printing. After that, he used any and all 'messy' materials and never looked back. We need to 'catch' all the children, whatever it takes.

Quiet reflection

Resources

- carpet squares, material, chairs, cushions
- tape recorder/CD player
- tapes/CDs – songs, stories, rhymes, sound games
- books – reference and fiction
- comics and child magazines
- dictaphones
- soft toys
- language and mathematics games that cannot be blown by the wind
- small motor-skill games
- writing and drawing materials

Remember

- Some children find it easier to look at books, write, etc. outside.
- This area will need adult input just as any other area does.
- Regularly change what is in the box (different story stimuli).
- Dictaphones are good for encouraging children to speak and to speak to an audience. They can report on what is going on outside, similar to a TV presenter.

Figure 3.5a–3.5c
Making a dragon. This took most of the morning and involved many children, some for a short period of time, and some for much longer. It drew observers and suggestions. It was a cold day, but everyone was wrapped up well.

Figures 3.6a–3.6c
Children are able to write and are confident enough to know that many materials can be drawn and written in snow and frost, for example. These children have access to writing materials and confidently pick out what they need for their activity.

Phonics

Alongside the structured phonics sessions outside is the natural place to practice talking and listening for children. Skipping rhymes, ring games and songs, ball games with song and rhyme can all be played to aid both movement and language.

For example:

> Puffer train, puffer train,
> Noisy little puffer train
> If you're going to the sea
> Puffer train oh please take me
> F, F, F, Sh, Sh, Sh, ch, ch, ch, ch, ch, ch, ch, ch
> Noisy little puffer train.

This practises those initial sounds brilliantly.

Old MacDonald's farm is about sounds, and actually the vowels can substitute 'e i e i o' and instead can be sung 'a e i o u'.

When using sand and water, the possibilities with regard to language are vast; for example:

bob	**flow**
bump	**stream**
bubble	**surge**
ripple	**swell**
wavy	**slosh**
trickle	**splash**
spring	**babble**
shiny	
gush	
rush	

What beautiful words these are.

See Bilton (2013a) for more examples of how to develop phonological understanding in the outdoors.

Other bays

Outside can be used for just about any activity. These could include:

- storytelling;
- singing;
- music;
- movement;
- mealtimes;
- snack; and
- adult-led teaching sessions.

Case study

Except on very cold days, this setting provides a snack outside but it is a self-service style and not at a dictated time. In this way, snack becomes a part of the curriculum, children learn to read a menu, pour, wash up, make choices and judge when they are ready for a snack. This approach does not cut into the timetable, but enables children to interrupt their own flow. The significance of it being outside means that all children, even the more reticent, experience being outside. Those unsure children can watch the proceedings outside while being 'protected' behind the veil of eating and drinking. What the staff members then find is those children become confident about outside and then venture out at other times.

Questions

- Do the outdoor activities enable children to become involved in representing their ideas in a written form?

- Are children encouraged to plan their play for the next day and predict what will happen next in the activity?

- Are children encouraged to listen to each other?

- Are children encouraged to use mathematical language in a precise way as they work?

- Are you mathematically literate?

- Are children encouraged to make pre-and post-plans of their constructions?

- What do you do for the children who tend to play with a limited number of activities? Does it matter?

- Is the storage area safe so children can use equipment and resources as they wish?

4 Creating a workable playing environment

In this chapter, I will be looking at the environment, the 'how' of the educational equation, particularly time, space, resources and adults. The how of education brings children and curriculum together, but, done badly, the how part of the equation can undo any good work you are trying to achieve. Constantly, we need to evaluate what we are putting in, in terms of effort and money, and decide whether we are reaping enough rewards from that effort; if not, things need to change.

Resources

How you arrange resources and what you make available to the children says a lot about what sort of practitioner you are. If children cannot access resources freely, this suggests you do not

Figure 4.1a
Although inside, this epitomises how children can make the most of nothing! A cardboard tube, two margarine pots and a sweet tin lid, and this child is racing in his car!

Figures 4.1b–4.1d
Arrangement of resources so they are accessible to children and easily put away. The all-weather suits are hung outside where children can collect and put them on for themselves.

Figure 4.1e
This is an imaginative set-up created by the adult – some buckets with cement and a broom handle fixed in place, pieces of plastic and material attached to the broom handles, ropes. It is very simple and quite cheap, but has the potential to really inspire some children.

trust them. If there are very few resources, you do not care about them. If children are not allowed to mix resources and equipment, you do not want them to think.

For children to think through and follow up ideas, they need to be able to put their thoughts into actions, so if they need the blocks, plus cones, broom handles, material and some large leaves to make an idea in their head real, they should be able to do this.

In a home where play is valued, children will gather resources from many areas – bathroom, kitchen, living room, garden. When children can select resources, they are able to make informed choices, make decisions and have control over the direction of play, and this in turn improves the quality of play and learning.

Free and found resources are about the most useful, with a scattering of bought ones. Be specific when asking parents for resources, and do not be palmed off with their rubbish! They often want to donate some plastic monstrosity; say no!

What you might want to ask for are old lined curtains, pieces of carpet to warm up the ground for planting, cardboard boxes for imaginative play and bits of guttering for science experiments. Try Scrapstores (www.childrens–scrapstore.co.uk) for recycled leftovers and Freecycle (www.freecycle.co.uk) to get free materials. Looking through the images in this book will demonstrate this; some of the pictures will show resources that have cost nothing.

Get rid of as many tacky coloured plastic items as possible. Just because the children are young does not mean we have to insult them with highly coloured items. They are discerning enough to appreciate beautiful natural colours and objects. And we can teach them to appreciate the wonders of the natural world.

Bikes

Three-wheeler bikes, funny little bubble cars, can cause more trouble than they are worth. The following is a description of what typically happens in a setting where bikes are used, particularly if outside play is allotted a set short period of time halfway through the session.

Children who wish to go on the bikes will want to get outside as fast as possible and may not get suitably dressed for the weather, just so they are out first. No one has said to the children that the blue bike is the best, the yellow bike not so good, and if you are on the green bike you are just a lower form of life. But this seems to be the attitude that prevails in every setting where bikes are simply put out en masse and children are left to get on with them. The story continues with children trying to stay on the bikes for as long as possible, not willing to share. When a child is taken off a bike, he or she will spend all his or her time trying to get back on the bike. Children may even act immorally to get a bike back: pushing others out of the way, pretending they have not had a turn on the bike already. Staff members end up policing, by organising who has a turn next, who has been wronged and who should be punished. This behaviour occurs day after day after day.

This is poor, stereotypical play and needs to be stopped. What appears to be happening is that the high-status toy gives high status to the owner, and so the child's self-esteem goes up. Apart from the status, children like bikes because of the speed; they enjoy the feeling of moving fast and the feeling of fear. When the bike has to be given up, the child's self-esteem goes down, they can feel lost and their only redress is to try to get on a bike again. There may be an analogy here with real cars; some people feel better behind the wheel of a car and their self-esteem goes up. Most worrying is that children are not having deep and meaningful conversations with adults, simply closed and basic dialogue that will not develop language and thinking.

What can be done?

- Most importantly, raise children's self-esteem so it stays high and is not affected by the possession or not of a toy.

- Think about not having three-wheeler bikes.

- Have two-wheeler bikes. There is no reason why under-fives should not be able to learn the skill of riding a two-wheeler.

- When three-wheeler bikes are used, insist that children have to have a truck tied to it, or only buy three-wheeler bikes with attachments.

- Fit an old bike, without the wheels, to a heavy wooden frame and make an exercise bike.

- Set up play scenarios that involve bikes (for example, fast food delivery, ice cream 'van', flower delivery, supermarket delivery, postman, etc.). Fit a box to the front of the bike to facilitate this.

- Make sure adults get involved with the children's play, providing ideas and extending what children can do. It is very difficult to hold a conversation with a child who is simply whizzing by.

- Plan carefully for outdoor learning, offer a variety of activities and be outside for as long as possible each day.

- If you do consider your children need pedalling opportunities, then offer bikes in a particular place and/or a bike time. In this way, the bikes do not encroach on others' play.

Figure 4.2
Four-wheel trucks are more inclusive than bikes, and are important for heart and lung exercise, spatial awareness and embedding of the transporting schema.

Figure 4.3a
Children have access to these all-weather suits and have the space to put them on. They are playing dens outside, although it is a day of intermittent rain.

All-weather access

Outdoor play is not a summer pursuit. Poor weather can be used as an excuse not to go out, but all weather conditions can be exploited.

How can this be achieved?

- Change the attitude so that instead of, 'It's raining so we can't go out', have, 'It's raining, great, how can we use this for the benefit of the children?' or 'compensate for the constraints, exploit the opportunities'. Weather happens all the time!

- Have a weather chart, check it every day, and predict what the weather might be like tomorrow or next week. Exploit the Web by checking the weather every day with the children using, say, the Met Office website. Or use two weather websites and compare the weather.

- Heavy rain is really the only weather feature that stops you going outside. Do not timetable outdoor play for a particular time, and then you can go out when it is not raining. Extreme cold and wind do not stop you going out, but may limit the amount of time outside.

- Keep boxes of spare clothing (gloves, hats, caps and long-sleeved T-shirts), coats for all types of weather (cold and wet) and footwear (such as wellington boots). Finding out which boots fit can be a great mathematical exercise for children.

Case study

A unit found the classroom was getting too cold when free flow was happening, as the door was one that either had to stay open all the time or closed all the time. The problem was solved by hanging plastic strips at the door, as used on heavy-duty butcher freezers. The plastic is translucent, so figures could be seen as they approached the doorway.

- Explain to parents, and keep explaining, that children will be working outside and why.

- Have an all-weather policy, discussed and agreed by all the staff.

- Put together a development plan for shade and shelter. This could involve making shelters from materials draped over A-frames or over four secured poles, or draped between a fence and some other structure. Large umbrellas and pop-up tents offer a degree of shelter. Plant trees and quick-growing shrubs to provide shade. A reasonable-sized tree should offer protection within three years. Consider having some form of more permanent shelter built, such as a veranda or pull-out shade or pergola covered in thick plastic, canvas or bamboo sheeting (see Figure 4.3b). In this way, children can go out whatever the weather. But do not then make the mistake of using the veranda as a storage space, which leaves nowhere to play.

- In very poor weather, free access to the outside may not be suitable for all, but small groups can be taken out.

Figure 4.3b
A veranda/covered way. This has drop-down doors so sections can be closed or open to the elements.

Case study

Children are allowed to go out in the wet and mud, and incidentally learn how to walk on muddy grass without falling over, but are expected to clean the boots when they come in. The routine is that each foot with a boot on is placed in a bowl of soapy water, scrubbed down with a long-handled brush and then left to dry on the side. Children learn to step back into their shoes once the operation is complete. Children are capable of so much if we give them the opportunity.

- There needs to be a variety of surfaces outside, and although grass is very attractive, one can have too much. Some settings seem to have areas that collect rainwater, but these can be made less boggy by buying all-weather covering materials. Alternatively, train children to wear wellingtons but clean them when they come inside.

- Make up weather boxes for wind, sun, rain, snow, etc. Together, collect resources, books, songs and rhymes that are relevant to that particular weather feature.

The sun

Children need access to light and sunlight, not only for emotional reasons, but, very importantly, for the synthesis of vitamin D. We had eradicated rickets from this country, but it is now back. Do not lather children in factor 50 suncream; this does not give protection, this causes risk to health. The manufacturers of these creams make a lot of money scaring everyone, but children need direct access to some sunlight and light every day. Of course, we have to be sensible, but we can do this by limiting time in the sun, offering quality shade, but also allowing the skin to experience the sunlight.

Fixed equipment

Many settings have fixed equipment; that is, equipment attached to the ground that cannot be moved. The difficulty with this type of equipment is that it can be limiting in helping children to learn. There are only a finite number of movements that can be made on it and it cannot be moved, changed or adapted to suit children's interests. After a while, children actually become bored by the equipment and use it less and less. Beautifully designed fixed equipment can stretch the designer's imagination, but can do little for a child's. Sometimes, a fixed piece of equipment can become a magnet for poor behaviour.

What can you do?

- If you have fixed equipment, do not just leave it, but try to make it different, add to it, change it. For example:

  - The wooden house – make sure this is well resourced. Change the focus regularly as you would any imaginative play area. It could be a florist, a railway station, a shop counter or a music corner.

  - Climbing apparatus – use it to attach equipment for the movement of water, such as guttering, pipes and tubing. Make it into a den using material and ropes.

- Consider attaching A-frames, planks or material to fixed climbing equipment. It may be that you will need to find a home-made source of planks, as the rungs on fixed climbing apparatus can be wider than the average plank hook-up.

- It may be that you need to actually remove the fixed piece of equipment or part of it. I can think of a setting who realised that just one part of the climbing apparatus was problematic, causing poor behaviour, and had it removed and the play changed.

Figure 4.4
An example of creating a set-up/a stimulus for play, particularly for those children who struggle with coming up with ideas for play.

Figure 4.5a
Tyres and planks are a walkway today. But tomorrow, who knows – this equipment could be used to create a campfire.

Figures 4.5b–4.5c

An example of an excellent piece of fixed equipment – a sandpit under cover, so it can be used all year round. If the space is tight inside, then this can be an ideal way to provide the essential social, scientific and linguistic stimulus of sand outside every day. This canopied area also has sufficient room to house resources and a role-play area.

In and out available simultaneously

Outside and inside need to be available at the same time, so children can move freely between the two areas.

Having all the children outside at once, for a timetabled play, causes the following problems:

- little or no planning goes into the area, and therefore learning is by chance;

- a few or the same toys are put out day after day;

- children tend to run around, very unfocused and 'manic';

- disagreements occur between children about the few toys that are available;

- staff members spend time dealing with disputes, not teaching children, so the only things that are learned are things the children teach themselves;

- opportunities for conversations linked to thinking and learning are lost;

- children behave in the same way every day;

- some children dominate the area;

- some children are scared of being outside;

- staff members do not enjoy being outside; they see it as a time for a break and a chat and to survive;

- children can behave quite badly and can become bored; and

- children do not learn to concentrate, persevere or think.

This is not good education, and I am almost inclined to say that it is not worth going out if this is the scenario. However, it is possible to change things by making the outdoor learning environment available at the same time as the indoor environment, planning it well and involving children in high-quality interactions. When out and in are simultaneously available, there is a huge difference in behaviour, approach and learning. Children are not manic; they are purposeful in their play, considerate of others, happy, less frenetic, wanting to learn, playing with different children and learning much more.

Suggested improvements

- To ensure that both indoor and outdoor play are used well and neither disturbs the other, outside should be available as soon as possible after the children come to the setting. Do not use outdoor play as a carrot for being good during the rest of the session.

- It is difficult to put a time limit on how long children should be outside. However, generally, there needs to be at least an hour's play outside to ensure children have time to follow their interests, learn to concentrate and persevere, and teaching plans can be carried out. It needs to be available whenever free-flow indoor play is offered.

- If outside has to be timetabled and cannot be alongside indoor play, then make sure that:

  ▸ it happens at the beginning of the session;

  ▸ you are outside for as long as possible;

  ▸ you incorporate outside into the plans;

Case study

In a nursery school, the children were able to go out for over an hour, free flowing between in and out. However, this was not until the children had been inside for about 40 minutes. About 10 minutes before the doors were opened, some children started to move about the room, clearly not doing anything in particular. Then, more children joined in and the feeling in the room became one of anticipation and unrest. I was disturbed by this movement, as clearly were other children. Finally, one of the children who had got up initially said, 'Can we go out?', to which the reply was, 'No, not yet, it's not quite time.' By the time the doors were opened, the majority of the children had been disturbed. These children could not tell the time and yet they could feel amounts of time. They were unable to concentrate, waiting for outdoor play to happen.

> - it is well resourced and equipped; and
> - adults work and play with the children.

- Always make sure the planning is for both indoors and outdoors; do not complete separate planning sheets.

Combining play outside and in

Having two environments – one in and one out – is not the end of the story. We also need to use the environment that best fits the learning and to encourage play and learning to occur between the two. They cannot be seen as two separate environments, otherwise learning is lost. For example, children are better off gardening outside, but, without a greenhouse, would be better starting plants off inside. One may be looking at the properties of water, which moves on to explaining the concepts on a grander scale, and so outside is best used. Drawing can start inside, but the light is much sharper outside, so it would be of benefit to complete pictures outside. Children could be using prepositions to describe a Lego construction, but could actually move using those prepositions outside – going over A-frames, along planks, into and out of hoops and so on. A construction or building could be planned and drawn inside, but actually created outside. In this way, skills of preparation, imagination, design and creativity are used, followed by interpretation, construction, adaptation and redesign.

Suggestions

- You could have a sorting office outside and a post office inside; a launderette inside and a washing line outside; a florist inside and a garden centre outside; a café outside and a house inside; a garage receptionist inside and the workshop outside. Of course, all these imaginative areas could be outside, but having one in and one out gives children the opportunity to link the two areas themselves.

- Children can be encouraged to make objects at the technology table inside to use in their play outside. Children do not need fancy bought signs, menus, binoculars, computers or flowers; all of these things can be made by the children.

- Although children will have resources to be used outside placed outside, they should also be able to access resources inside. It may be they want to play with a particular game outside, which is usually stored in the classroom. Unless there is a practical difficulty, such as it may blow away, children should see the outside as much as a workshop as inside and that resources can be used in either area.

- Involve the children in talking about outside and how it can be used. Let them participate in setting up equipment outside – they will be very imaginative in what can be used effectively outside. We can become very narrow in our thoughts; children tend not to have such blocks.

Case study

It was a cold December day and the ground and water were frozen. Children went out as usual, noted the conditions and talked about it. The adult focused their attention to the frost on the table, comparing its properties to the frost on the ground.

Then they noticed the frozen pond. This prompted one child to find out how thick the ice was, and she started to hammer it with a block. The child and adult chatted about why the water was frozen and this led to a decision to set a large bucket of water on the ground to see if it would also freeze. The child collected a large bucket and filled it from the outside tap. The adult carried the water, as it was quite unstable.

A lot of discussion ensued about where to put this bucket. Would it better here or there to freeze quicker, so it did not get disturbed, and so on.

A decision was finally made and the adult suggested tentatively as to whether the child thought it might be quite a good idea to write a sign to say do not disturb.

It was then decided that, maybe as a comparison, a small pot of water should be placed outside to see if it froze, and if it took a longer or shorter amount of time to freeze than the larger pot. Initially, the small pot was placed next to the large pot, but for some reason the child insisted the small pot actually had to be inside the large pot. She then felt a need to guard her experiment!

Learning that occurred was scientific, alongside the associated language. The child was using her hands to manipulate the tap and bucket. She was given a reason to write, and read that writing. Her desire to know and understand was aroused and acknowledged (see Figures 4.6a–h).

Figures 4.6a–4.6h (pages 81–3)
This child had an interest and fascination with the ice. The adult was instrumental in ensuring her knowledge and understanding was developed.

Layout

Outside cannot be left as an open and empty space. As each of us makes a house into a home, so each outdoor space needs to be made in to a place (Tovey 2007). A place special to that setting. Make sure the space is divided into areas, not rigidly, but flexibly, through the arrangement of resources and equipment or a chalk line. Children need exploratory and enclosed secret areas, which can be created through the considered planting of shrubs and trees. Keep branches low so children have to bend down and creep, as these are useful motor skills. This is also a way of creating a quiet bay or an area for imaginative play. Do not overfill the space so it becomes cramped and cluttered.

Suggestions

- Get children involved in class and school projects so they can discuss what they would like and physically help create the ideas. For example, making a water feature, creating a wild area, planting up shrubs, and adding bark chippings and top soil – children can be involved with all these projects.

- Think about creating a hill house or tree house, as children can feel safe high up and it gives a very different visual perspective.

- Rather than have a bike track, have a pedestrian track, which makes for an interesting walk, with different textured surfaces – bricks, half-logs, pebbles, AstroTurf, bark chippings, large stones. Children enjoy balancing on the different textures and it makes them want to explore the far reaches of an area. Along the track can be different types of planting herbs, aromatic plants, colour-combined plants and so on. This style of pathway will elicit great conversation.

Questions

- Do you talk to parents about the value of outdoor play?

- Do you see rain as a problem or just another weather feature?

- What do you need to do to the environment to make sure all children have equality of opportunity and access?

- Is the fixed equipment a magnet for poor or stereotypical behaviour?

- Is the fixed equipment planned for? Do you use it in different ways?

- Do children really have access (and know they do) to a whole host of resources and equipment?

Figure 4.7

Children are making porridge with sand in the wooden house and under the climbing frame. They had bowls, sand and a place. They discussed and imagined. They got on and they chatted. This is an example of children being given the freedom to mix and match so that they can follow their interests and understanding to take them to a new place of knowledge and understanding.

5 Where do we go from here?

In this chapter, I will be looking at how to make changes or develop the outdoor area by sharing a number of ideas already put into practice.

I cannot believe that it is such a long time since the Brent Project, but despite that, the blueprint we put together for developing outdoor provision still stands. What follows is the description of how to go about making changes to outdoor practice, whatever your needs.

Case study

In 2003, the Early Years Service in Brent began a project to raise the profile of outdoor play in their settings. Practitioners from the maintained and non-maintained sector were invited to attend an outdoor conference and then indicate an interest in being part of the project to improve outdoor provision and commit themselves to a year-long project, during which they would examine practice and record their progress. Three sessions, one per term, were planned to support the practitioners. The early-years team supported the settings making changes, and the final session together culminated in a celebration of achievements and successes.

If you want to make changes, then advice from that project, which, incidentally, Brent repeated year on year, is as follows:

- structure the outdoor learning project;
- identify the issues;
- create an action plan, development plan and timeline (be realistic – see pages 88–9);
- involve colleagues;
- include children in the process;
- get support from whomever you can;
- involve the community;
- take photographs all the time;

- understand and be able to verbalise what children can learn when outside;
- understand the role of the adult;
- appreciate that you do not need a fortune to make significant changes;
- be flexible;
- expect problems;
- expect unexpected solutions; and
- celebrate.

Everyone involved with the project felt the changes had significantly improved outdoor provision for young children. These are some of the improvements:

- instances of ill health lessened;
- children became more robust;
- children were able to judge risk more accurately;
- children became more independent;
- children developed an 'I can' approach;
- flexible, open-ended materials gave children the opportunity to learn more about the process of negotiation and decision-making;
- children with English as an additional language became more confident communicators;
- the fear some children had of living creatures diminished;
- practitioners became more aware of the potential learning opportunities outside;
- practitioners noted reduced number of conflicts;
- over time, parents appreciated what the benefits of working outside were as children came home 'refreshed, not frustrated'; and
- over time, parents appreciated the need to send their children suitably dressed.

Making more of what you know and have already

Sometimes, we can be so keen to come up with yet another idea that we forget to make the most of what we have already or have thought of. For example, transporting is a very standard schema/repeatable behaviour/activity of young children. And yet, do we really make the most of this in our outdoor settings?

Action Plan

What do you want to develop?	Why?	How?	Resources and cost	Who does what?	How long?	Evaluation and evidence

Individual Educator Audit

List 3 positive areas/aspects/activities of outdoor play in your setting:

1.

2.

3.

List 3 areas for improvement in outdoor play in your setting:

1.

2.

3.

Timeline for developing priorities from action plan

Month	Action

Source: "Learning Outdoors: Improving the quality of young children's play outdoors". David Fulton Publishers. ISBN 1 84312 350 9
Copyright © Helen Bilton, Karen James, Jackie Marsh, Anne Wilson and Maggie Woonton 2005
www.fultonpublishers.co.uk

Case study

One early-years unit decided to focus, rather than on activities, on one of the repeatable behaviours to structure their provision. This is an example of one such focus. The unit first made observations of children and found they would transport other children, dolls, puppets, and objects – commercial, made and found. They found that children's play would often stop at the point of lack of stimulus of materials. So they decided to add collections of: stones, shells, twigs, pebbles, bark, cork, leaves, gravel, sea glass, cones, beads, wool, string and feathers, all in separate ice cream containers. This added significantly to the resources available to children for transporting and mixing. They already had wooden community plaything pushchairs, trolleys, low trucks, buckets of various sizes, scoops, and child-size trowels.

They then considered, rather than setting up activities, what mathematical learning could come from the transporting. And these are some of the ideas they had:

- sharing out – the stones, cones, etc. into different trucks and places;
- swapping – 'I'll give you three stones for six feathers'; or, when there was lack of space in a trolley or container, discussing about swapping a smaller object for the larger ones (this is all to do with ratio);
- counting materials in and out of containers (this is the basic use of number);
- discussing the weight and size of objects; and
- arranging the materials around the garden.

They thought in terms of children's play being in terms not of one-offs, but of long-term projects to be revisited day after day, and thereby this gave the opportunity to use the language of time.

Some of the language was as follows: **empty, full, push, pull, heavy, light, arrange, rearrange, more/less mix, double, halve, share, in, out.**

With these resources and this knowledge about an area of development, they were able to quite easily both start to role model with the materials and also, with ease, intervene with the play to move it forward.

Figure 5.1

A balance made by a dad, from some old blocks and some buckets. Home made is often so much better than bought, as it fits with what you really need, as opposed to what the manufacturer thinks you want. Something like this balance is so useful when children are transporting materials.

Making changes

To develop or change the outside area takes a good deal of discussion and consideration before action. Where you start will depend on where you are at the moment. It could be: collecting resources into named boxes; assessing adult behaviour; getting rid of resources and gathering more versatile materials; or changing the timing of when children can access the outdoor teaching and learning environment. Changes need to be manageable and measurable. They also do not cost a fortune. Here is an email correspondence between Nicki Turner and myself about developments she had been making.

From: Nicky
To: Helen
Sent: 14 January

Hi Helen

I have had a request from you to make a connection on LinkedIn. However, I have forgotten my password, so cannot access it! You actually joined the seminar I was running on outdoor and maths at the 2006 Leicestershire EY conference. I work at Christ Church and St Peter's Primary in Mountsorrel and lead the EYFS unit (which has almost 90 children).

I have introduced a completely child-led, play-based curriculum, and am currently developing the outdoors, which you may be interested in. At the moment, it is just concrete, so there are going to be some big changes, including the introduction of:

- superheroes gym and training centre;
- mud kitchen;
- sand kitchen;
- Stomp-style music area;
- Zen garden;
- water play with three different waterfall features;
- tree-climbing and woodland area;
- large outdoor home with upstairs;
- dens and huts;
- art- and mark-making
- hills, bridges and tunnelling system;
- vegetable garden; and
- woodworking shed.

The bikes and bedlam trikes are going, and the plastic toys have already gone. The children have chosen what they wanted and helped plan where it should all go.

If you need any real examples of EYFS practice, in particular development of the outdoors, I am more than happy to share what we are doing with you.

From: Nicky
To: Helen
Sent: 14 January

At the moment, the outdoor area is just tarmac and fencing, but it is going to undergo a complete transformation. The planning stage is complete and we are now deciding on the time frame for completing all of the various parts. The first area to be developed will be the tunnels, hills, bridges and large-scale construction. Interestingly, we are restricted by the fact that we are the access route for the fire engine and the tractor that comes to mow the school field, so you may like to see how we get round this limiting factor.

It is going to be brilliant and I cannot wait to get it all sorted for the children.

I have a working committee that includes children, parents, the premises officer, business manager and myself. The equipment used for the project will largely be recycled materials and donations from the local community. We have very little money in the school so almost everything will be made from recycled materials and will be constructed by our wonderful caretaker Arthur. Arthur is also going to work with the children once a week in the woodworking shed making things such as go-karts.

This week, I am going to create a Gantt chart for the development of the outdoors.

From: Nicky
To: Helen
Sent: 27 January

I am creating a presentation for the school Big Vision Day all about how we want to develop the EYFS garden. Jack in my class is desperate for a caravan. Last week, he started to make a papier mâché one. So, I am getting him a real caravan. A parent in my EYFS garden develop group is going to get one for us from a recycle and swap place in Leicestershire; apparently there is a website for it.

Exciting stuff.

From: Nicky
To: Helen
Sent: 28 February

The outdoors has only just started to be developed. We have been having a lovely time in the mud kitchen today [see Figures 5.2b–d] and have been making adventure playgrounds out of lorry tyres and large plastic pipes. The children have been so excited to go into the mud kitchen. We have had many donations of pots, pans, sieves, etc. from home. Yesterday, I observed the children creating the kitchen. It was fab, as they were moving cabinets and troughs from one side of the garden to the other. They just did it independently, so nice to watch. And watching a group of 4 year olds flip and roll lorry tyres and move them into the desired place was pretty amazing. This was done with chants of 'roll it' and 'teamwork, teamwork'. I have had to do a big load of washing tonight, though, as I have a number of pairs of rough kit jeans that have been severely mud-kitchened!!!

Figure 5.2a Trying out being a stuntman and gymnast.
Figure 5.2b The mud kitchen – a cheap and versatile resource.

Figure 5.2c The mud kitchen – scientific and imaginative.
Figure 5.2d The mud kitchen – easily created anywhere in the garden.

From: Nicky
To: Helen
Sent: 1 March

I've got £4,000 to spend on our area. Most of the items will come from donations, but I do need to buy some special plastic to make the superhero gym kick bags out of, and I need some wood for various things. I am trying to get a cheap caravan too. A parent has sourced one in Skegness and is looking at how we can get it to Leicester.

My best buy so far has been 12 straw bales from the local farm [see Figure 5.2e]. This cost us £30. The children use them for a variety of things. They have built castles and adventure playgrounds, combining things such as pallets and bricks to make walkways and slides. The children have learnt how to transport the bales by flipping them. They are so proud of themselves when they move the bales, as it is a challenging job for a 4/5 year old to lift and flip a bale all by themselves.

Constructing with the bales often requires teamwork, so they have been a great resource for cooperative play and also problem-solving.

Because the bales are not static, the children can create a number of things with them and move them around where ever they like. This loose-parts construction for adventure playgrounds is amazing because it means that there is more than one answer, more than one way of doing something.

After watching a video of Damien Walters (stuntman and gymnast, check him out on YouTube), the children have wanted to develop their gymnastics skills.

They have been perfecting some very daring jumps from bales, including giant leaps involving mid air twist and jumps with extended arms and legs. The bales were placed on the long ends in parallel to create equipment for dips, bridges and balancing. The most daring skill so far that some children are highly motivated to perfect are the backward walkovers off the bales. There are a couple of girls who want to do this over and over. The physical adventure that they have on the bales is amazing to watch. The skill the children have developed is incredible, and it is brilliant to watch children challenge themselves and develop even more advanced ability with balance, strength and agility.

The learning gained from the straw bales gymnasium seems far more than when they take part in the typical PE gymnastics in the hall. I have observed children doing things that I never see in PE inside. The outside gym and the PE hall have a totally different feel. Children are much more daring outside. There seems to be less restrictions outdoors. The atmosphere is totally different, as it is learning through self-selected play rather than that directed by the teacher. In the outside gymnasium, children can express themselves more and can explore their abilities and limits more. Inside, the PE is more controlled, so children are not able to be so audacious and daring.

The other day, they stacked the bales so they were at an angle; they then did rolls down the slopes. I have got my children doing backward walkovers off the bales, rolls down slopes and cartwheeling into handstands up against walls. The height that some children get when jumping from the bales is also high enough for a tuck summersault. I have recommended that some parents get their children to a proper gymnastics club as they seem to have a bit of a talent.

Figure 5.2e
Straw bales – 12 for £30, incredibly versatile.

Figure 5.2f Looking for the Big Bad Wolf.
Figure 5.2g Teamwork.

The children have also been using the loose straw combined with bricks and wooden blocks to create small world play areas. A popular theme has been making a house for a mouse. This was after reading a story called George and the Dragon. The children combined materials making sure that the mouse house had an entrance, windows and a cosy living area. The children became very protective of the mouse house and had to ensure that the houses did not get damaged, as this would not be fair for the mouse. A lot of thought went into the construction, and I observed the children verbalising their thoughts to themselves and to others while constructing the houses.

We have been reading the story of the Three Little Pigs at school. The other day, we had a letter arrive from the Big Bad Wolf. In the letter, the wolf said that he does not like our school and that he is going to blow it down, which will be doing everyone a favour as he has heard that school is rubbish anyway. The children have been a bit worried about this, but, as the school is made from bricks, they know that it will not get blown down. But, just in case, the children have been making traps for the wolf outside. They have found his house, which is on the other side of the school fence among some trees [see Figure 5.2f]. A number of dens have also been made to hide away from the Big Bad Wolf. I have really enjoyed watching the children bring this story to life in their outdoor play over the past few weeks. They have been getting really into it, and to them it is DEADLY SERIOUS!!!!

Feel the enthusiasm of Nicky; it is infectious! This is someone who wants to really develop practice for her children. But, very importantly, note the level of planning and thought that has gone into this. Significant changes take time and effort, flexibility and adaptation. Also note that Nicky is not expecting a huge amount of money to make the changes and actually is keen to source as much recycled materials as possible.

Clever people with a love of outside, great knowledge and an ability to explain complicated things simply need to work with young children.

The staff members who work with young children need to be the cleverest in the land. The questions posed by 4 year olds can be so tricky. 'Why doesn't my birthday fall on the same day every year?' is a hard one to answer anyway, but to then answer it to the satisfaction of a 4 year old is incredibly difficult. Those with the greatest understanding plus the ability to explain in simple terms are who we need working with young children. In secondary schools, when pupils suggest they do not know what to do with their lives, they are often directed towards childcare. But on two counts this is troublesome. First, often these are pupils who will not chose to go on to higher education. Second, what is this saying to everyone about how we value early-years education?

Anne Crook has a PhD from Oxford in Zoology and she ran an Explorers Club on a Friday afternoon at the local school for Year 2 children. The area used was not large, but because Anne knew what she was doing, she was confident to let the children explore the space, and so the area felt much larger than it is. What is magical about Anne is her depth of subject knowledge, her understanding and her ability to explain. What follows are Anne's thoughts about her Explorers Club.

Anne's ramblings

I have always had a passion for natural history, and with an academic background in Zoology rapidly becoming a fading memory, I wanted to do something in my local community that would encourage others to get outdoors and start investigating the natural world around them. For me, the obvious place to start this venture was with a group of people that I felt were not as naturally engaged and active in the outdoors as they had been in my generation – children!

Watching my 5-year-old son grow up, I have been constantly amazed by his natural curiosity about the world around him, a curiosity that, unfortunately, as we grow up, I believe many of us either bypassed or failed to draw upon because of so many other pressures and demands on our time and minds. I am a passionate believer that you need to care for and understand your local environment if you are to truly understand how the world 'works', and the role that the human race has, and can play, in sustaining life on earth. But if you do not even know what animals and plants are living in your own proverbial backyard, then why would you care if wildlife on the other side of the world is threatened with extinction, particularly if you may never get to see any of it in your lifetime?

Alongside my desire to draw upon children's natural curiosity, I also wanted to provide local children with opportunities to 'just run free' outdoors and to experience nature, warts and all:

- to get muddy, wet and dirty;

- to know what happens if you brush up against a stinging nettle or a bramble (and know what to do about it!);

- to take some risks and to have the confidence to engage in activities that might be beyond their normal 'comfort zones';

- to climb trees and build dens;

- to find 'minibeasts';

- to work together to solve problems; and

- to make their own fun!

I was very fortunate in the timing of my ideas for a new 'Explorers Club' because my son's local primary school, Chilton Primary, was just at that time starting to investigate the possibility of creating a Forest School within its grounds. The school is located on the edge of the Chilterns and has multiple habitats on its doorstep, as well as a 'wild' area and pond within its grounds, making it an ideal focus for exploration. Combined with a head teacher who is an active supporter of outdoor learning, I was very fortunate to essentially be given a free reign to run my Explorers Club and to work with a class (Year 2) across an academic year.

The Explorers Club took place every Friday afternoon for 90 minutes (irrespective of the weather) and each week the Year 2 teacher would select a group of six children to come with me to the 'wild' area of the school so that, over time, all the children in the class had several opportunities to be part of the club. Each week, I would bring in various

Figures 5.3a The space looks a lot bigger than it is, but you do not need a massive forest to feel away from others.

Figures 5.3b Children made observations, did lots of talking with Anne and with each other, sometimes to explain, check, come to an agreement, or to be amazed.

Figures 5.3c Making decisions.
Figures 5.3d Children spent time coming to decisions as to what the insects were. Some spent time lost in the books, storying and journeying.

wildlife guidebooks and equipment to sample and observe 'minibeasts' (nets, binoculars, observer sheets, measuring instruments, etc.) but I would ask the children what they would most like to do that afternoon and how they might like to use the various pieces of equipment that I had brought in (if at all!). Activities were therefore led by the children's interests, were open-ended and, not surprisingly, ended up being different most weeks: some weeks, the children wanted to see if they could find '20 different bugs' in the afternoon and identify them using my guidebooks; other times, the children enjoyed identifying and counting the numbers of different birds they could see in the school grounds; other times, they wanted to build dens, climb trees or make 'houses' for insects (in the case of tree-climbing, I ensured the children undertook their own form of self 'risk assessment' to see whether or not the tree they proposed to climb would indeed hold their weight safely – and, of course, in case of doubt, I would intervene to ensure their safety).

A thread across all the weeks was my request for the children to record their animal and plant findings in a notebook, which I gave to the children each week to take charge of and to enter their records (see Figures 5.3b, c and e). It did not take long before the different groups became quite competitive with one another, and questions such as '*how many bugs did the explorers find last week?*' were common, leading to flurries of activity to ensure they found and recorded more animals and plants than the previous week's group! At the end of the term, I printed a summary of most interesting plants and animals the class had found in the school grounds for them to take home to show their families (see Figures 5.3g and h) so that the children could share their explorations.

I did not want the Explorers Club to feel like an extension of school or to be overtly structured with the aim of 'learning something' per se (although of course I hoped that they would learn something!), but I did feel the need to have a set of ground rules, which I reminded the children of at the start of the club each week.

Explorers Club 'rules':

- If I am talking to the group, I need everyone to listen to make sure we all stay safe.

- Respect the animals and plants that we find.

- Mud and dirt are OK ('that is why we have washing machines!').

- Have fun!

I feel privileged to have been able to run the Explorers Club, which, as well as getting the children 'back to nature', was also successful in helping to support the development of the school's new Forest School. I am extremely grateful for the open-mindedness of all the staff at the school and their trust in my abilities and my vision for the Explorers Club. Staff feedback has shown that the children really enjoyed the freedom of being outdoors and readily engaged with their 'local patch', which is a very promising start for the new Forest School and the exciting activities that the teachers have planned for the children in the years to come.

Even now, one year on, the children who were in the Explorers Club regularly come up to me after school to tell me that they have spotted an interesting bug in their garden, or that they have been building a den in the park and have taken part in various wildlife initiatives.

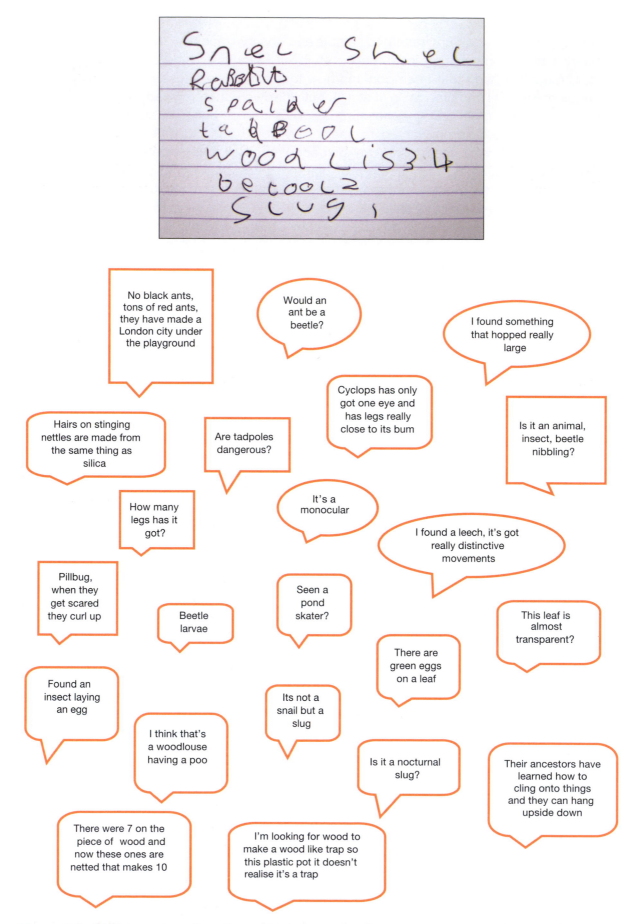

Figures 5.3e Children wrote easily as the need was apparent and necessary.
Figures 5.3f Snippets of conversation caught at one Explorers Club afternoon.

Year 2 Explorers Club: The School Pond Area

Explorer Group	Date	What did you find?
1 Josh Thomas David Tate Scott Oli	16th September 2011	Frogs Woodlice Moths Spiders Ladybirds Snails
2 Eve Harry D'Arcy Finn Natasha Alice Tommy	23rd September 2011	Rabbits Spiders Ladybirds Beetle Woodlice Snails Ants Worms Slugs Fly
3 Callum Scarlett Owen Freya Megan Cameron James	30th September 2011	Beetles Moth Earwig Velvet mite Spiders Ladybirds Woodlice Snails Ants Flies Lichen
4 Evie Chiara Luke Lars Ciera Emily Rosamund Lestyn	14th October 2011	Spiders Woodlice Centipedes Worms Ants Snails Slugs Ladybirds Flies Velvet mites Earwig Shield bug

Figure 5.3g A list of the plants and animals found at Explorers Club.

Figure 5.3h Some of the animals and plants found by Year 2 at the school pond area (Sep–Oct 2011).

Source: www.wikipedia.org; www.buglife.org.uk/; www.wildengland.com/wild-animals/small-creatures/insects/moths.

What a great place to finish a book about outdoor teaching and learning – with someone who adores everything about being outside, is not afraid of the freedom, the inhabitants(!), or the weather, and is so enthusiastic that children she has worked with are still sharing their discoveries. Anne 'knows her stuff'. We need more people in early years like that.

Resources and contacts

- **A-frames/trestles**

  These can be bought from Brian Clegg (see below) and from companies such as Olympic Gymnasium Services.

  www.olympicgymnasium.com (accessed 2 April 2013)

  They also sell mats, planks, etc.

- **Art project using ice**

  www.artfulparent.com/2012/07/melting-ice-science-experiment-with-salt-liquid-watercolors.html (accessed 2 April 2013)

- **BBC Gardening**

  www.bbc.co.uk/gardening/gardening_with_children (accessed 2 April 2013)

  This is full of ideas, resources, information and projects for children.

- **Brian Clegg**

  Regent Mill, Regent St, Rochdale, Lancashire, OL12 0HQ.
  Tel: +44 (0)1706 666 620
  www.brianclegg.co.uk (accessed 2 April 2013)

  Suppliers of A-frames, ladders, trucks, pushchairs and platform trolleys.

- **Charity shops and parental contributions**

  Help parents to appreciate the value of outdoor play and they will help with supplying resources.

- **Community Playthings**

  Robertsbridge, East Sussex TN32 5DR
  Tel: +44 (0)800 387 457
  www.communityplaythings.com (accessed 2 April 2013)

  A supplier of extremely well-made and long-lasting equipment for all aspects of play. In particular, playcubes, carriages, wheelbarrows and blocks (unit and hollow, Figures 3.2a–3.2h). The staff members are very friendly and helpful.

- **Countryside Management Services**

  Unit B2, Durham Dales Centre, Castle Gardens, Stanhope, County Durham DL13 2FJ
  www.cms-ne.co.uk/index.htm (accessed 2 April 2013)

  This organisation has educational packs and programmes and will give advice.

- **DIY and furniture stores** have very useful materials. It is often a case of just wandering through them and being inspired.

- **Freecycle**

  www.uk.freecycle.org (accessed 2 April 2013)

  'The worldwide Freecycle Network is made up of many individual groups across the globe. It is a grassroots movement of people who are giving (and getting) stuff for free in their own towns. Freecycle groups match people who have things they want to get rid of with people who can use them. Our goal is to keep usable items out of landfills. By using what we already have on this earth, we reduce consumerism, manufacture fewer goods, and lessen the impact on the earth. Another benefit of using Freecycle is that it encourages us to get rid of junk that we no longer need and promote community involvement in the process.'

- **Key Hole Garden**

  www.organicgarden.org.uk/urban-micro-farming/keyhole-gardens (accessed 2 April 2013)

  A brilliant way of creating a compost heap and garden all in one!

- **Met Office**

  www.metoffice.gov.uk/education (accessed 2 April 2013)

  This has experiments that can be used with young children. The site is useful for following weather patterns, resources and ideas for teachers to use, and for children to access.

- **NES Arnold**

  www.nesarnold.co.uk (accessed 2 April 2013)

  Suppliers of wooden climbing frames.

- **Plastic door strips**

  www.pvc-strip-curtain-warehouse-plastic.co.uk (accessed 2 April 2013)

  Lightweight plastic transluscent strips can be hung at the door to keep heat in and cold out.

- **Reading International Solidarity Centre (RISC)**

  www.risc.org.uk (accessed 2 April 2013)

  They work with schools to promote global issues, and promote sustainable development, human rights and social justice. The website is a useful source of information and advice.

- **Royal Society for the Protection of Birds (RSPB)**

  www.rspb.org.uk/ourwork/teaching/catalogue/early_years.aspx (accessed 2 April 2013)

  Lots of free resources, information and ideas.

- **Royal Society for the Prevention of Accidents (RoSPA)**

  RoSPA House, 28 Calthorpe Road, Edgbaston, Birmingham B15 1RP
  www.rospa.com/leisuresafety/playsafety (accessed 2 April 2013)

  This organisation has useful publications regarding safety, risk assessment and standards, but not everything relates to educational settings.

- **Science experiments**

  www.parentingscience.com/preschool-science-experiment.html (accessed 2 April 2013)

- **Storage sheds**

  There are a plethora of types. Make sure they are made of wood, as the plastic ones tend to warp and they look awful. Plain wood is much kinder to the eyes.

- **Tarpaulin**

  www.tarpaulinsdirect.co.uk (accessed 2 April 2013)

  This is really useful for covering things and for using as something to sit on.

- **Treeblocks**

  The Old Barn, Vale Farm, Mays Lane, Barnet, Hertfordshire EN5 2AQ
  Tel: +44 (0)800 970 1600
  www.treeblocks.co.uk (accessed 2 April 2013)

  A source of wooden blocks.

- **Woodland Trust**

  www.woodlandtrust.org.uk (accessed 17 November 2013)

  A source of information, ideas and free resources.

- **Woodwork**

  Children can use woodwork tools as long as they have the correct tools and are taught properly. Woodwork benches may need to be cut down so they are the right height for the children.

Bibliography

BILTON, H. (2010) *Outdoor Learning in the Early Years Management and Innovation*, 3rd edition. Abingdon: Routledge.

BILTON, H. (2012) 'The type and frequency of interactions that occur between staff and children outside in Early Years Foundation Stage settings during a fixed playtime period when there are tricycles available'. *The European Early Childhood Research Journal* 2(3), 403–21.

BILTON, H. (2013a) 'Miss I want that bike'. In **FEATHERSTONE, S.** *Getting Ready for Phonics – L is for Sheep*. London: Bloomsbury Publishing, pp. 105–12.

BILTON, H. (2013b) 'Setting the scene for children – initiated learning out of doors'. In **FEATHERSTONE, S**. *Supporting Child-initiated Learning: Like Bees, not Butterflies*. London: Bloomsbury Publishing, pp. 73–9.

BILTON, H., JAMES, K., MARSH, J., WILSON, A. and WOONTON, M. (2005) *Learning Outdoors Improving the Quality of Young Children's Play Spaces*. London: David Fulton Publishers.

BLURTON-JONES, N. (1967) 'An ethological study of some aspects of social behaviour of children in nursery school'. In **MORRIS, D.** *Primate Ethology*. London: Weidenfeld & Nicolson, pp. 347–68.

CARTWRIGHT, P., SCOTT, K. and STEVENS, J. (2002) *A Place to Learn*. London: PDA Design and Advertising.

CLEMENTS-CROOME, D. J., AWBI, H. B., BAKO-BIRO, Z. S., KOCHHAR, N. and WILLIAMS, M. (2008) 'Ventilation rates in schools'. *Building and Environment: The International Journal of Building Science and its Applications* 43(3), 362–7.

DEPARTMENT OF EDUCATION AND SCIENCE (DES) (1989) *Aspects of Primary Education: The Education of Children Under Five*. London: HMSO.

EDGINGTON, M. (2003) *The Great Outdoors: Developing Children's Learning Through Outdoor Provision*, 2nd edition. London: British Association for Early Childhood Education.

FEATHERSTONE, S. (2003) *The Little Book of Outside in All Weathers*. Leicestershire: Featherstone Education.

GALLAHUE, D. L. and DONNELLY, F. C. (2003) *Developmental Physical Education for All Children*. Champaign, IL: Human Kinetics.

HEALTH AND SAFETY EXECUTIVE (HSE) (2012) 'Case 92 – press story said health and safety is a barrier to children playing conkers, using skipping ropes or climbing trees'. Available at: www.hse.gov.uk/myth/myth-busting/2012/case092-children.htm (accessed 25 January 2013).

HOLLAND, P. (2003) *We Do Not Play With Guns Here: War, Weapons and Superhero Play in the Early Years.* Maidenhead: Open University Press.

KATZ, L. G. and CHARD, S. C. (1989) *Engaging Children's Minds: The Project Approach.* New York: Ablex Publishing.

MCLEAN, S. V. (1991) *The Human Encounter: Teachers and Children Living Together in Preschools.* London: Falmer Press.

MATTHEWS, J. (2003) *Drawing and Painting: Children and Visual Representation.* London: Paul Chapman Publishing.

NICHOLSON, R. (2001) *Planning for Foundation Stage Learning.* London: Wandsworth Borough Council.

OUVRY, M. (2000) *Exercising Muscles and Minds: Outdoor Play and the Early Years Curriculum.* London: The National Early Years Network.

PELLEGRINI, A. (1988) 'Elementary school children's rough-and-tumble play and social competence'. *Developmental Psychology* 24(6), 802–6.

SHIELD, B. M. and DOCKRELL, J. E. (2008) 'The effects of environmental and classroom noise on the academic attainments of primary school children'. *Journal of the Acoustical Society of America* 123(1), 133–44.

STEPHENSON, A. (2003) 'Physical risk-taking: dangerous or endangered?'. *Early Years* 23(1), 35–43.

SYLVA, K., MELHUISH, E., SAMMONS, P., TAGGART, B., TOTH, K., SMEES, R., DRAGHICI, D., MAYO, A. and WELCOMME, W. (2012) *Effective Pre-school, Primary and Secondary Education Project (EPPSE 3–14) Phase: Influences on Students' Development from Age 11–14. Research Report DFE-RR202.* London: Department for Education.

TOVEY, H. (2007) *Playing Outdoors: Spaces, and Places, Risk and Challenge.* Maidenhead: Open University Press.

WALSH, P. (1991) *Early Childhood Playgrounds: Planning an Outside Learning Environment.* Mt Victoria, NSW: Pademelon Press.